REFLECTIONS IN THE LIBF
SELECTED LITERARY ESSAYS 19

LEGENDA

LEGENDA is the Modern Humanities Research Association's book imprint for new research in the Humanities. Founded in 1995 by Malcolm Bowie and others within the University of Oxford, Legenda has always been a collaborative publishing enterprise, directly governed by scholars. The Modern Humanities Research Association (MHRA) joined this collaboration in 1998, became half-owner in 2004, in partnership with Maney Publishing and then Routledge, and has since 2016 been sole owner. Titles range from medieval texts to contemporary cinema and form a widely comparative view of the modern humanities, including works on Arabic, Catalan, English, French, German, Greek, Italian, Portuguese, Russian, Spanish, and Yiddish literature. Editorial boards and committees of more than 60 leading academic specialists work in collaboration with bodies such as the Society for French Studies, the British Comparative Literature Association and the Association of Hispanists of Great Britain & Ireland.

The MHRA encourages and promotes advanced study and research in the field of the modern humanities, especially modern European languages and literature, including English, and also cinema. It aims to break down the barriers between scholars working in different disciplines and to maintain the unity of humanistic scholarship. The Association fulfils this purpose through the publication of journals, bibliographies, monographs, critical editions, and the MHRA Style Guide, and by making grants in support of research. Membership is open to all who work in the Humanities, whether independent or in a University post, and the participation of younger colleagues entering the field is especially welcomed.

ALSO PUBLISHED BY THE ASSOCIATION

Critical Texts
Tudor and Stuart Translations • *New Translations* • *European Translations*
MHRA Library of Medieval Welsh Literature

MHRA Bibliographies
Publications of the Modern Humanities Research Association

The Annual Bibliography of English Language & Literature
Austrian Studies
Modern Language Review
Portuguese Studies
The Slavonic and East European Review
Working Papers in the Humanities
The Yearbook of English Studies

www.mhra.org.uk
www.legendabooks.com

STUDIES IN COMPARATIVE LITERATURE

Editorial Committee
Dr Duncan Large, British Centre for Literary Translation,
University of East Anglia (Chair)
Dr Emily Finer, University of St Andrews
Dr Dorota Goluch, Cardiff University
Dr Priyamvada Gopal, Churchill College Cambridge
Professor Timothy Mathews, University College London
Professor Wen-chin Ouyang, SOAS, London
Professor Elinor Shaffer, School of Advanced Study, London

Studies in Comparative Literature are produced in close collaboration with the British Comparative Literature Association, and range widely across comparative and theoretical topics in literary and translation studies, accommodating research at the interface between different artistic media and between the humanities and the sciences.

ALSO PUBLISHED IN THIS SERIES

Reflections in the Library

Selected Literary Essays 1926–1944

ANTAL SZERB

EDITED BY ZSUZSANNA VARGA
TRANSLATED BY PETER SHERWOOD

LEGENDA

Studies in Comparative Literature 46
Modern Humanities Research Association
2016

Published by Legenda
an imprint of the Modern Humanities Research Association
Salisbury House, Station Road, Cambridge CB1 2LA

ISBN 978-1-78188-461-4 *(HB)*; 978-1-78188-462-1 *(PB)*

All rights reserved. No part of this publication may be reproduced or disseminated or transmitted in any form or by any means, electronic, mechanical, photocopying, recording or otherwise, or stored in any retrieval system, or otherwise used in any manner whatsoever without written permission of the copyright owner, except in accordance with the provisions of the Copyright, Designs and Patents Act 1988, or under the terms of a licence permitting restricted copying issued in the UK by the Copyright Licensing Agency Ltd, Saffron House, 6–10 Kirby Street, London EC1N 8TS, *England, or in the USA by the Copyright Clearance Center, 222 Rosewood Drive, Danvers MA 01923. Application for the written permission of the copyright owner to reproduce any part of this publication must be made by email to legenda@mhra.org.uk.*

Disclaimer: Statements of fact and opinion contained in this book are those of the author and not of the editors or the Modern Humanities Research Association. The publisher makes no representation, express or implied, in respect of the accuracy of the material in this book and cannot accept any legal responsibility or liability for any errors or omissions that may be made.

Trademark notice: Product or corporate names may be trademarks or registered trademarks, and are used only for identification and explanation without intent to infringe.

© *Modern Humanities Research Association 2016*

Copy-Editor: Charlotte Brown

Translated with the support of:

MINISTRY OF
FOREIGN AFFAIRS AND TRADE
OF HUNGARY

HUNGARIAN BOOKS
AND TRANSLATIONS
OFFICE

PETŐFI
LITERARY
MUSEUM

Balassi
Institute

CONTENTS

FOREWORD

Galin Tihanov

Antal Szerb (1901–1945), a Hungarian-Jewish intellectual and a representative of a brilliant generation of Central-European essayists between the two World Wars, has left behind a body of prose (his novels have been available in English for some time) that also includes valuable work in comparative literature. With Legenda's edition, the Anglophone reader now receives, for the first time, the opportunity to read significant selections of Szerb's literary criticism and scholarship.

Szerb's major works as literary critic and scholar are his *History of Hungarian Literature*, a book of essays on the novel, and his magnum opus, a *History of World Literature* (1941); all three have been translated into German. The first two books appeared in the 1930s, with Szerb's discussion of the novel reflecting major developments in literary studies at the time, foremost György Lukács's theory of the novel and Károly Kerényi's work on myth and narrative. Szerb's account of Hungarian literature is demonstrably free of nationalist bias; he seeks to realign Hungarian literature with the evolution of literatures in the West, leaving behind the parochialism of the largely populist schemata that see Hungarian literature as a sanctuary for home-grown uniqueness. His book of essays on the novel (some of them also translated in the current edition) is a testimony to his ability to recognize wider patterns and modes of relevance behind individual texts and authors. To this, one should add his writings on English literature, not least the first ever study of William Blake in Hungarian, and also his outline of the history of English literature (1929).

But it is Szerb's intervention in the emerging inter-war Central-European debate on world literature that makes him our contemporary and is likely to claim the attention of literary scholars today. The stage had been set by Mihály Babits (1883–1941), another Hungarian intellectual of the highest calibre, whom Szerb admired and learned from. Babits, a poet, a prose writer, and a literary critic, was a central figure in *Nyugat* [West], the modernist literary and cultural journal of liberal orientation, to which Szerb also became an important contributor. In the mid-1930s, Babits published his *History of European Literature* (translated after World War Two into German and Italian), in which he proffered his own nostalgic reflection on world literature. Unlike the exponents of the currently prevalent Anglo-Saxon discourse on world literature who largely believe world literature to be the offspring of major recent developments (globalization and transnationalism), Babits understood it to be tied to cultural and political formations that preceded the nation-state. It was Greece and Rome that exemplified for him the space of world literature, sustained by the two great shared languages of European culture, Greek and Latin. With the arrival of the modern nation state (and especially since its rise across Europe in the nineteenth century), world literature was gradually diminished and, eventually, made impossible by the unrelenting strife and bickering amongst the small states of Europe, each of them championing its own language. Unabashedly Eurocentric, Babits's version of world literature is indicative of later attempts, notably by Ernst Robert Curtius, to reconstruct the unity of European culture by recasting it as a phenomenon of the past that holds lessons for the future.

Szerb continues Babits's line whilst also taking his distance from it. Like that of Babits, Szerb's own narrative is unapologetically Eurocentric. World literature, Szerb insists, comprises the literatures in Greek and Latin, the Bible, and the vernacular writing in French, Spanish, Italian, English, and German. He also follows Babits in his choice of writings on which the stamp of canonicity had been embossed; Szerb's answer to the question what constitutes canonicity is proto-Gadamerian: the canon is that which tradition names as canonical. Thus the compass of world literature is severely circumscribed: it is the body of writing that has been relevant to Europe (Szerb briefly discusses American literature and the classical literatures of Islam, but not of China and Japan, although they, too, had an impact on European literature at a later stage), and that has become truly canonical, i.e. significant beyond a period or a single (European) culture. At the same time, unlike Babits, Szerb is less inclined to lament the collapse of world literature since the arrival of the nation state and nationalism. While he recognizes the loss of shared languages, he is more sanguine about the role played by national cultures: his discussion of Russian and Scandinavian literatures directs our attention to the national as a gate through which previously unnoticed literatures are drawn into the orbit of world literature.

Methodologically, Szerb is beholden, yet not without reservations, to Oswald Spengler's theory of cultural cycles, in which civilizations are subject, ineluctably, to growth and decline (Szerb explicitly acknowledges Spengler's framework early on in the book). For Szerb, this is evident in the rise of two conflicting stylistic (often also ideological) lines in the evolution of European literatures. This principle of antagonistic duality, very much part and parcel of the analytical toolkit of art history and literary studies at the time (to which Mikhail Bakhtin also pays its dues in his essays on the novel), informs Szerb's discussion of Romanticism and Realism, which he places at the centre of his history. Romanticism is prepared by the growth of the Gothic and Baroque, and it then exfoliates to give rise to Symbolism, various Modernisms, and a whole plethora of other post-Romantic *écritures*. At the other end of the spectrum one finds Realism, which Szerb takes as evidence of European literatures having entered a phase of decline. Realism, just as Romanticism, is only the end product of the evolution of an entire stylistic formation that mirrors a certain outlook and system of values; this formation comprises Classicism and the Enlightenment, with their allegedly homogenizing and trivializing insistence on the supremacy of the rational, proportionate, and decorous. Still, following Lukács's vision of a new synthesis of epic and novel, Szerb departs from Spengler by considering the great examples of rejuvenation of Realism during the inter-war period, in which the epic returns (often with a renewed presence of myth at its heart) to nestle within the novelistic; amongst the best illustrations Szerb furnishes is Thomas Mann, notably championed at the time by both Lukács and Kerényi.

Szerb's work on world literature is an insightful and stimulating exercise in cultural and intellectual history; at the same time, it is a cautionary tale about the difficulties we are bound to face when trying to ponder the scope of world literature today and the extent to which it lends itself to historical conceptualization. The tenor of Szerb's work was unmistakably humanistic; he believed that world literature produces better readers and, through this, better human beings. This project of amelioration might sound excessively optimistic, but its ambition reminds us that our own search for a renewed relevance for literary studies and the humanities today ought to be aiming high.

London, July 2016

TRANSLATOR'S NOTE

Peter Sherwood

Brief notes on some of the literary figures mentioned by Antal Szerb and likely to be less familiar to the Anglophone reader will be found on pp. xvii–xviii. Footnotes added by either the translator or editors have been placed within square brackets, so as to distinguish them from Szerb's original footnotes.

I would like to express my thanks to the other chief contributors to this volume, Professor Ágnes Péter (Budapest), Professor Elinor Shaffer, FBA (London/Cambridge), and Dr Zsuzsanna Varga (Glasgow/Oxford), for their invaluable comments on early drafts of the translations. I owe a special debt of gratitude to my erstwhile student Mrs Eileen Zwalf, for her sustaining friendship over many years; her unquenchable enthusiasm for all things Hungarian, which invariably blossoms into lively discussion whenever we meet, has greatly benefited these texts. Naturally, none of those mentioned is responsible for any errors or imperfections that no doubt remain.

London, Easter 2016

ACKNOWLEDGEMENTS

This edition of Antal Szerb's essays is in large part a by-product of a long-standing collaboration between the series *The Reception of British and Irish Authors in Europe* (Bloomsbury Press) and a number of Hungarian literary historians. The editor is particularly indebted to the editorial team consisting of Professors Ágnes Péter, Elinor Shaffer, Peter Sherwood and Galin Tihanov, who all contributed to the volume in a variety of ways (see below).

For generous financial assistance and encouragement the editorial team is grateful to Dr Zsuzsanna Szabó of the Publishing Hungary Foundation, Budapest; Dr Zoltán Jeney of the Translation Support Fund of the Hungarian Books and Translations Office, Budapest; Dr Zoltán Balog, Hungary's Minister for Human Resources; and Mr Gergely Pröhle, lately of the Ministry of Human Resources, currently Director-designate of the Petőfi Literary Museum, Budapest. We would also like to thank the National Trust (Swindon) for permission to use the cover image and the Petőfi Literary Museum for permission to use Szerb's photograph.

We are all especially grateful to Dr Graham Nelson of Legenda for supporting the project throughout its long gestation.

The contributors to this volume were as follows:

*Ágnes Péter, Professor Emerita and formerly Head, Department of English Studies, Eötvös Loránd University, Budapest (ELTE)

*Elinor Shaffer, FBA, Professor, School of Advanced Study, University of London

*Peter Sherwood, Emeritus Professor of Hungarian Language and Culture, University of North Carolina at Chapel Hill

Galin Tihanov, George Steiner Professor of Comparative Literature, Queen Mary University of London

*Dr Zsuzsanna Varga, School of Social and Political Sciences, University of Glasgow

The volume was edited by Zsuzsanna Varga; the essays were jointly selected by those marked with an asterisk; the translator was Peter Sherwood; Galin Tihanov contributed the Foreword; and the Introduction was the work of Ágnes Péter.

z.v., Glasgow, December 2016

NOTES ON THE PRINCIPAL LITERARY FIGURES MENTIONED IN THE ESSAYS

Endre Ady (1877–1919), one of Hungary's greatest lyric poets, a champion of literary modernity, whose highly original language and distinctive symbolism characterized his often revolutionary themes.

János Arany (1817–1882), one of the finest Hungarian poets and critics, noted for his historical poetry and ballads, especially his *Toldi* trilogy. His translations of three of Shakespeare's plays are prized nineteenth-century classics of Hungarian literature.

Mihály Babits (1883–1942), outstanding Hungarian writer, poet, and man of letters, second in importance and influence only to Ady (q.v.) among the first generation of the westward-looking writers of the important journal *Nyugat* [West].

Vissarion Belinsky (1811–1848), eminent Russian critic, often called the 'father of the Russian radical intelligentsia'.

Andrei Bely (1880–1934), Russian novelist, poet, and literary theorist, author of *Petersburg*, regarded by Vladimir Nabokov as one of the twentieth century's four greatest novels.

György Bessenyei (1746 or 1747–1811), poet and playwright, leading figure of the Enlightenment in Hungary, strongly influenced by Voltaire.

Johann Jakob Bodmer (1698–1783), German-Swiss writer, poet, and academic, an opponent of French pseudo-classicism and of Gottsched and his school. See also Breitinger (q.v.).

Paul Bourget (1852–1935), French novelist, poet and critic, particularly noted for his novel, *Le Disciple* (1889).

Johann Jakob Breitinger (1701–1776), Swiss writer and philologist, best known for *Thesaurus historicae helveticae* (1735), which he co-authored with Johann Jakob Bodmer (q.v.). In his influential work *Critische Dichtkunst* (1740) he rejected imitation of nature as a poetic principle in favour of the creative imagination.

Salomon Gessner (1730–1788), Swiss painter and poet, whose *Idyllen* (1756 and 1772), in particular, were very popular and widely translated in the second half of the eighteenth century.

Friedrich Gundolf (1880–1931), influential literary scholar, poet, and academic in Weimar Germany.

Albrecht von Haller (1708–1777), Swiss anatomist, physiologist, naturalist, and poet, author of *Odes sur les Alpes* (1773).

Ilya Ilf (1897–1937) and Evgeny Petrov (1903–1942), two Russian satirical authors of the 1920s and 1930s, who did much of their writing together.

Mór Jókai (1825–1904), probably Hungary's most beloved and prolific storyteller, a historical novelist comparable with Scott. Over a dozen of his novels have appeared in English; in the nineteenth century he was practically the only Hungarian writer known to the Anglophone world.

Baron Miklós Jósika (1794–1865), writer and journalist, author of the first Hungarian Romantic (and historical) novel, *Abafi* (1836).

Baron Zsigmond Kemény (1814–1875), Transylvanian Hungarian politician and Hungary's most important historical novelist after Mór Jókai (q.v.).

Károly Kerényi (1897–1973), Hungarian classical scholar, one of the founders of the modern study of Greek mythology. Szerb, in his novel *Utas és holdvilág* [Journey by Moonlight] (1937), modelled some features of Rudi Waldheim on Kerényi.

Károly Kisfaludy (1788–1830), army officer and painter, one of the founders of the Hungarian drama. Brother of Sándor Kisfaludy (q.v.).

Sándor Kisfaludy (1772–1844), perhaps the first Hungarian Romantic poet, brother of Károly Kisfaludy (q.v.).

Ferenc Kölcsey (1790–1838), Hungarian poet, critic, orator, and liberal politician, author of the Hungarian national anthem, *Himnusz* (1823). See also Vörösmarty (q.v.).

György Lukács (1885–1971), Hungarian Marxist philosopher, aesthete, critic, and historian of literature, one of the founders of Western Marxism.

Imre Madách (1823–1864), Hungarian poet, author of the great dramatic poem *Az ember tragédiája* [The Tragedy of Man] (1861), which may be compared in ambition to Goethe's *Faust*. The most notable translation into English is that by George Szirtes (1989).

Ákos Pauler (1876–1933), distinguished Hungarian philosopher, defender of metaphysics against logical positivism.

Sándor Petőfi (1823–1849), Hungary's national poet, who died on horseback fighting the Habsburgs' Russian allies at the end of the failed Hungarian War of Independence, 1848–1849. A rhymed English translation by John Ridland (1999) of his popular 'folk epic' *János vitéz* (1845) is accessible online as *John the Valiant* at <http://magyarmegmaradasert.hu/in-english/multi-topic/1682-janos-vitez-john-the-valiant> [accessed 9 July 2016]

Boris Pilnyak (1894–1938), Russian writer critical of urbanism and mechanized society.

Aleksey Remizov (1877–1957), Russian Modernist writer of bizarre works and appearance.

Frigyes Riedl (1856–1921), noted Hungarian essayist, critic, and historian of literature, best remembered for his monograph on János Arany (q.v.).

Mihály Vörösmarty (1800–1855), one of the greatest Hungarian Romantic poets and dramatists of the Age of Reform, author of *Szózat* [Appeal] (1836), the 'second Hungarian national anthem'. See also Kölcsey (q.v.).

P.S.

TIMELINE OF MAJOR WORKS
BY ANTAL SZERB

This timeline draws on UNESCO's *Index translationum* and the national libraries and national union catalogues of the United Kingdom, Hungary, France, Spain, and Germany, and the Library of Congress. A particularly helpful source has been Csaba Nagy's *Szerb Antal bibliográfia* (Budapest: PIM, 2001), covering national as well as international aspects up to 2001. I should like to take this opportunity to thank Paul Barnaby for his willingness to share his bibliographical expertise.

The timeline lists Szerb's works according to the date of their first publication. No effort was made to trace the bibliograhical details of his work published after 1945, as this information is widely available in library catalogues. The column 'Critical work on Szerb' lists only major publications in Hungarian and English. Periodical reviews of his work have been omitted. The column 'In Translation' covers the translations of Szerb's work into the major European languages, and only in print rather than digital format. Reprints of translations are noted where such information is available.

Z.V.

1. During Szerb's Lifetime

Year	Original Work	In Translation
1926	Essay: *Stefan George*	
1927	Essay: *A magyar újromantikus dráma* [The Hungarian New Romantic Drama]	
	Essay: *Az udvari ember* [The Book of the Courtier]	
1928	Essay: *William Blake*	
1929	Essay: *Az ihletett költő (Berzsenyi Dániel)* [The Inspired Poet: Dániel Berzsenyi]	
	Essay: *A magyar preromantika* [Hungarian Pre-romanticism]	
	Essay: *Az angol irodalom kistükre*	[A Brief Survey of English Literature]	
1930	Essay: *Vörösmarty-tanulmányok* [Studies on Vörösmarty]	
1934	Monograph: *A magyar irodalom története* [The History of Hungarian Literature]	
	Novel: *A Pendragon legenda* [The Pendragon Legend]	

1935	Short stories: *Szerelem a palackban* [Love in a Bottle] Short story: *Budapesti útikalauz mars-lakók számára* [A Martian's Guide to Budapest] Essay: *A kuruckori költészet* [Kuruc (early 18th century) Poetry]	
1936	Essays: *Hétköznapok és csodák* [The Everyday and the Miraculous], on French, English, American and German novels after WWI Essay: *A harmadik torony* [The Third Tower]	English — 'Love in a Bottle' (the title story from the collection) in *Hungaria: An Anthology of Short Stories by Hungarian Authors*, trans. Lawrence Wolfe, London: Ivor Nicholson and Watson
1937	Novel: *Utas és holdvilág* [The Traveller and Moonlight]	
1939		German — *Die Suche nach dem Wunder: Umschau und Problematik in der modernen Romanliteratur*, Amsterdam and Leipzig: Pantheon
1941	Short stories: *Madelon, az eb* [Madelon, the Dog] Essay: *Captain John Smith in Transylvania* Monograph: *A világirodalom története* [The History of World Literature]	
1942	Monograph: *A világirodalom története* (2nd, revised edition)	
1943	Novel: *A királyné nyaklánca* [The Queen's Necklace]	
1944	Poetry: *Száz vers* [100 Poems]	

2. After Szerb's Death

Year	Original Work	Critical Work on Szerb	In Translation
1946	Essays: *Gondolatok a könyvtárban* [Reflections in the Library]		
1948	Essays: *A varázsló eltöri pálcáját* [The Magician Breaks his Staff]		
1963			English — *The Pendragon Legend*, trans. Lili Halápy, Budapest: Corvina
1964		Monograph: Poszler, György. *Szerb Antal pályakezdése* [Antal Szerb's Early Career]	Spanish — *Amor en el boleto*, trans. Lajos Tárkony in *Hungara vivo* no. 1 (periodical)

1965		French — *Madelon, le chien,* trans. Péter Komoly, Budapest: Corvina
1966		German — *Marie Antoinette oder Die unbeglichene Schuld,* trans. Alexander Lenard, Stuttgart: Goverts German — *Die Pendragon-Legende,* trans. Henriette Schade-Engl, Budapest: Corvina (also 1968, 1977)
1967		English — 'Madelon, the Dog' in *22 Hungarian Short Stories,* trans. Pál Morvai, Budapest: Corvina and London: OUP German — *Ex: Lustspiel in Drei Akten,* trans. Maria v. Keresztury (based on *Oliver VII*), Vienna: Molden
1968		German — *Liebe in Einmachglas,* trans. Joseph Sternberg, Budapest: Corvina
1972		German — *Oliver VII,* trans. Ita Szent-Iványi, illustrated by Rudolf Peschel, Berlin: Eulenspiegel-Verlag
1973	Monograph: Poszler, György. *Szerb Antal*	
1975		German — *Ungarische Literaturgeschichte,* trans. Josef Gerhard Farkas and Gabriele Farkas, Youngstown, OH: Franciscan Fathers
1989		Italian — *La leggenda di Pendragon,* translation and afterword by Bruno Ventavoli, Rome: E/O (also 1994, 1999)
1990		French — *La Légende de Pendragon,* trans. Natalia Zaremba-Huzsvai and Charles Zaremba, Aix-en-Provence: Alinéa

1992			French — *Le Voyageur et le clair de lune* trans. Natalia Zaremba-Huzsvai and Charles Zaremba, Aix-en-Provence: Alinéa
1994			English — *The Traveler*, translation and afterword by Peter Hargitai, New York: Authors Choice Press (also 1995, 2003, 2005, 2007)
1996		Memoirs, essays, letters: Wágner, Tibor (ed.) *Akitől ellopták az időt: Szerb Antal emlékezete* [A Man who was Robbed of Time: The Memory of Antal Szerb]	
1997	Essays: *A trubadúr szerelme: könyvekről, írókról 1922-1944* [The Love of the Troubadour: On Books and Writers 1922-1944], edited by Tibor Wágner		
1998			French — *La Légende de Pendragon* trans. Natalia Zaremba-Huzsvai and Charles Zaremba, Aix-en-Provence: Alinéa
1999	Short stories: *A fehér mágus: Elbeszélések* [The White Magician: Short Stories]	Essays and reviews: Wágner, Tibor (ed.) *Tört pálcák: Kritikák Szerb Antalról* [Broken Staffs: Criticism on Antal Szerb, 1926-1948]	
2000			Spanish — *El viajero bajo el resplandor de la luna*, trans. Judit Xantus, Barcelona: Del Bronce
2001	Diary: *Naplójegyzetek (1914–1943)* [Diaries: 1914–1943], edited by Mária Tompa with Ilona Petrányi	Bibliography: Nagy, Csaba. *Szerb Antal bibliográfia*. Budapest: PIM, 2001	English — *Journey by Moonlight*, trans. Len Rix, London: Pushkin Press (also 2002, 2007)

2002	Essays: *Összegyűjtött esszék, tanulmányok, kritikák* [Collected Essays and Reviews], 3 vols., including previously unpublished material	Essay: Poszler, György. 'The Writer who Believed in Miracles: Antal Szerb 1901-1945', *Hungarian Quarterly*, XLII, 167 (Autumn 2002) Memoirs, essays, letters: Wágner, Tibor (ed.) *Akitől ellopták az időt: Szerb Antal emlékezete* [A Man who was Robbed of Time: The Memory of Antal Szerb] (2nd, rev. edition)	French — *Le Voyageur et le clair de lune* trans. Natalia Zaremba-Huzsvai et Charles Zaremba, Aix-en-Provence: Alinéa
2003			Spanish — *La leyenda de los Pendragon* trans. Judit Xantus, Madrid: Siruela German — *Reise im Mondlicht*, trans. Christina Viragh, afterword by Péter Esterházy, Munich: Dt (also 2005, 2007, 2011)
2004			German — *Die Pendragon Legende*, trans. Susanna Grossmann-Vendrey, afterword by György Poszler, Munich: Dt (also 2005, 2007)
2005			German — *Das Halsband der Königin*, trans. Alexander Lenard, revised by Ernő und Renate Zeltner, Munich: Dt
2006			German — *In der Bibliothek: Erzählungen*, selected by György Poszler, trans. Timea Tankó, Munich: Dt German — *Oliver VII*, trans. Ita Szent-Iványi, unabridged, rev. edition, Munich: Dt English — *The Pendragon Legend,* revised trans. by Len Rix, London: Pushkin Press (also 2013)

2007			English — *Oliver VII*, trans. Len Rix, London: Pushkin Press (also 2013)
2009			English — *The Queen's Necklace*, trans. Len Rix, London: Pushkin Press (also 2011)
2010		Essay: Fülöp, Zsuzsa. 'The Image of Britain in Antal Szerb's Works', in *A tűnődések valósága: The Reality of Ruminating, Writings for Aladár Sarbu on his 70th Birthday*, Budapest: ELTE	English — *Love in a Bottle and other stories*, trans. Len Rix, London: Pushkin Press (also 2013)
2011			French — *Le Voyageur et le clair de lune*, revised trans. by Natalia Zaremba-Huzsvai and Charles Zaremba, Paris: V. Hamy German — *Gedanken in der Bibliothek: Essays über die Literaturen Europas*, selected and trans. András Horn, Basel: Schwabe
2012			French — *La Légende de Pendragon*, trans. Natalia Zaremba-Huzsvai and Charles Zaremba, Paris: V. Hamy Spanish — *El viajero bajo el resplandor de la luna* trans. Judit Xantus, Barcelona: Backlist
2013		Monograph: Havasréti, József. *Szerb Antal*	
2014			English — *The Third Tower: Journeys in Italy*, trans. Len Rix, London: Pushkin

2015		Essay: Farkas, Josef-Gerhard. 'Einführung zur Neuübersetzung von Antal Szerb, *Ungarische Literaturgeschichte*' <http://edocs.fu-berlin.de> [accessed 12 June 2016]	German — *Ungarische Literaturgeschichte,* trans. Josef-Gerhard Farkas and Gabriele Farkas, revised edition, Berlin: J. G. Farkas & G. Farkas English — *A Martian's Guide to Budapest*, trans. Len Rix, Budapest: Magvető
2016		Essay: Kiséry, András, and Zsolt Komáromy, 'World literature in Hungarian Literary Culture', in Kiséry-Komáromy-Varga. *Worlds of Hungarian Writing,* Madison, WI: Fairleigh Dickinson University Press Essay: MacDonald, Agnes Vashegyi. 'Antal Szerb's The Queen's Necklace: A True Story of Cross-Cultural Intersections in Hungarian Literature', in Kiséry-Komáromy-Varga, *Worlds of Hungarian Writing,* Madison, WI: Fairleigh Dickinson University Press	English — *Journey by Moonlight* trans. Peter Czipott, Richmond: Alma Classics English — *Traveler and the Moonlight,* revised trans. by Peter Hargitai, Bloomington, IN: iUniverse German — *Geschichte der Weltliteratur*, translated and edited by András Horn, afterword by György Poszler, Basel: Schwabe

Antal Szerb
Petőfi Literary Museum Photographic Collection

Antal Szerb:
The Passionate Reader

Ágnes Péter

In his review of Antal Szerb's monumental literary survey, *A világirodalom története* [History of World Literature], published in 1941, Gábor Halász, one of the most outstanding critics of Hungarian Modernism, defined Szerb's attitude to his subject as that of the 'passionate reader': his critical writings were, Halász claimed, confessions 'of a youthful fascination preserved deep in the mind, of a form of self-abandonment sweeter than love, of youth preserved in its virginity'.[1]

Probably it is indeed this impassioned tone of personal involvement that is the distinctive mark of the critical work of Antal Szerb (1901–1945), one of the most prolific writers and literary scholars of the interwar period in Hungary. In all the various fields of his career — he was a successful novelist, a literary historian of exceptional erudition and originality, a dedicated teacher, and a translator of literature and philosophy — he was motivated by the immense delight that he took in all forms of literature.[2] This delight found justification in his conviction that literature was one of the few things that represent permanence in our world of transient glories. In 1938 he published an autobiographical essay, *Könyvek és ifjúság elégiája* [An Elegy for Books and Youth], in which he said, 'If there is anything I am still certain about, if anything is left for me that can be described with the serious words "my sacred belief", it is a belief in the inevitable, humanly eternal nature of literature'.[3]

In Hungarian cultural memory Antal Szerb's persona has a poignant personal dimension. His career and painfully short life were organically connected with the tragic history of the region. After he had been conscripted as a Jew for labour service in 1944, he was deported to a concentration camp at Balf (today part of the town of Sopron) near the western borders of the country, where he was beaten to death on 27 January 1945. When the appalling barbarism of his end became known, his friend the literary historian Tivadar Thienemann said: 'Balf remains a never-healing, stinging wound in this country's memory'.[4]

In recent years Szerb has become the subject of renewed interest on the part of critics and readers alike in Hungary. To commemorate the centenary of his birth in 2001 the Budapest publishing house Magvető launched a serial edition of his literary and critical works, as well as his *Diary* and *Letters*, in a uniform jacket; and a magisterial critical study, *Antal Szerb*, came out in 2013 in which the author, the Pécs-based scholar József Havasréti, claims that the significance of Szerb the critic far exceeds his stature as a writer, and is actually much greater than hitherto thought.[5]

The present volume of Szerb's selected essays in English — representative of the originality as well as the allure of his critical mind — is presented to the English-speaking reader, who has already learned to appreciate the unique quality of Szerb's fiction, as a commemorative gesture to mark the seventieth anniversary of his untimely death in 1945.

Antal Szerb was born into a middle-class, assimilated Jewish family in 1901. The most formative historical experience of his generation, the collapse of the Austro-Hungarian monarchy in 1918, was described by Szerb in an autobiographical essay of 1938 as follows:

> The monarchy where I had been educated to become a citizen, the huge behemoth, vanished overnight, without too much notice taken of it and, unfortunately, without being mourned by anyone, as if it was a matter of the dissolution of a provincial choir; simultaneously our great example, Hohenzollern Germany, also vanished; and the *littérateurs* most in the know assured me that the great social class that had produced the culture to which I belonged, the bourgeoisie, was also to become in no time a distasteful historical memory. But I was too young to see the extent of the loss, to know that I had been crippled for life.[6]

The Peace Treaty of Trianon (1920) deprived historic Hungary of two-thirds of its territory and almost 60 per cent of its population, including 30 per cent of ethnic Hungarians.[7] Anxiety about the survival of Hungarian as ethnicity, language, and culture in the greatly reduced territory paved the way for nationalist-populist movements which used an ever more aggressively jingoistic and racist language; in the economic crisis of the 1930s, accumulating resentment found release in increasing hysteria in the face of the threat of both Nazism and Soviet Communism. In this atmosphere Szerb necessarily became more and more entangled in repeated attempts at self-definition. Eventually at the end of 1942 in his *Diary* he wrote: 'I have found my definition: I am a Jew whose mother tongue is Hungarian'.[8]

His intellectual development was amazingly fast ('I was a bespectacled infant'): we have his teenage essays on Thomas Mann and Ibsen's symbolism and they seem to anticipate some of the judgements of his mature assessment.[9] His public career began when *Nyugat* [West], the literary and critical journal which brought about the Modernist turn in Hungarian literature, accepted some of his poems for publication in 1921. This was followed two years later by the publication of his very ambitious essay on Stefan George, one of the cult figures for the critics of *Nyugat*. Szerb's position as a major critic of the time was secured by his literary history, *A magyar irodalom története* [History of Hungarian Literature], published in 1934, which was followed in the same year by the publication of his first novel, *A Pendragon-legenda* [The Pendragon Legend]. Both were greeted as expressions of a most original mind, provocatively challenging mainstream standards and taste. His survey divided public opinion in a radical way: it was enthusiastically received by the more progressive critical organs of the time; he was, however, severely censured by the more conservative media for blatantly subverting the dominant concept of traditional literary historiography as well as the received literary canon. He saw Hungarian culture as an organic part of the great European narrative, continuously fertilized and renewed by influences coming from outside. Rejecting the concept of indigenous paradigms he famously declared: 'whatever is most characteristically Hungarian is also most characteristically European. [...] to be a Hungarian today is not to be connected with the borders that delimit the state where you live but is defined by the culture you share'.[10] Szerb goes as far as to suggest that the nation-bound principles of traditional historiography resulted in isolation and provincialism, that the ancient history of Hungarian literature stemmed from a synthesis of Hungarian and European traditions, and that relative decay has always been due to a discontinuity in this synthesis. As time went on, anti-Semitic attacks on this literary history increased and eventually, in December 1942, the book was officially banned.

Despite the attacks Szerb continued to publish undaunted. In 1936 appeared a collection of essays, *Hétköznapok és csodák* [The Everyday and the Miraculous], on the new English, German, French, Russian, and American novel. In the same year his long essay, *Budapesti kalauz marslakók számára* [A Martian's Guide to Budapest] appeared in instalments in *Nyugat*, the following year his most ambitious novel *Utas és holdvilág* [Journey by Moonlight] came out, while his sweeping survey *A világirodalom története* [History of World Literature] appeared in three volumes in 1941. In 1943 he published *A királyné nyaklánca* [The Queen's Necklace], a 'feather-light historical essay' on the *ancien régime* disguised as a novel, or a novel disguised as an essay. At the end, in a desperate effort to preserve integrity, he compiled a multilingual parallel text anthology of one hundred poems, *Száz vers*, nearly all of which he claimed were 'connected in his memory with an experience of profound agitation'.[11] In the introduction to the selection Szerb writes: 'If poems survive, perhaps the essential thing survives. At least that is what some of us believe and that is what was taught by the wonderful Hölderlin: Was bleibet aber, stiften die Dichter'.[12] Some of his work appeared posthumously, including the comic novel *Oliver VII*, which, like all his other novels, defies categorization: a richly imagined joke, a parody of the thriller, or an exploration of identity as fate.

As is traditional for Hungarian literature, it was in German translation that Szerb the novelist first reached a non-Hungarian readership in the 1960s; he was later translated into all the European languages, and also into Hebrew. All his novels, as well as his collection of short stories, *Love in a Bottle*, were published by Pushkin Press between 2000 and 2015 in elegant translations by Len Rix, although other translators and publishers have also been attracted to his work. Everywhere the reception of Szerb's fiction has been enthusiastic: he has been recognized as a most important Modernist writer who actually anticipates post-Modernism. His combination of fiction and cultural history has led to comparison with Umberto Eco.[13] And everywhere the psychological realism, as well as the firm grasp on the potential of the novel as a genre, the simultaneous use of the traditional and the modern, of the magic and the scientific, of irony and scholarly seriousness, have been praised. George Szirtes wrote of the novel *Journey by Moonlight* in Len Rix's translation:

> There are elements of genuine paranoid vision, heavy surrealism, guidebook travelogue, Gothic horror tale, Chestertonian fantasy, intellectual debate and an uneasy social satire. [...] *Journey by Moonlight* is a burning book, a major book, one of those maddeningly uneven firework displays that serve as much for symptom as artefact.[14]

On the other hand the poet Jemma L. King called *The Third Tower*, his notes on his journey in Italy in 1936, also translated by Len Rix, a perfect book:

> Szerb's notes are not only a quality read but they should be more widely acknowledged given the trueness and tragedy of his story. 'Italy is mine, not Mussolini's. I am mine alone in my self-completeness' he writes defiantly. The author's quiet but resolute rectitude is heart-breaking in light of his biography [...] His notes, filled with courageousness and defiance in the face of emergent evil, seem timely reading material given the continent-wide swing to the far right in our recent European elections.[15]

Antal Szerb the critic, however, is little known outside Hungary. German-language publishers have shown some interest in his work, including the Basel-based Schwab Verlag, which brought out his critical essays in 2011 (*Gedanken in der Bibliothek: Essays über die Literaturen Europas*) and his survey of world literature (*Geschichte der Weltliteratur*) in 2016, but the present volume is believed to be the first to offer a selection from his critical work in English. What makes Antal Szerb's criticism worthy of the attention of an international readership is the extensive vistas his vision encompasses and his grasp of the great patterns in the history of European culture that give a great degree of unity to our shared values. In all his critical writings, including those on Hungarian authors and literary periods, individual issues are presented against a backdrop of the European scene and are discussed with the methods of comparative literary studies as established by Paul van Tieghem. His response to the ever-changing intellectual challenges posed by new critical trends was amazingly sensitive and creative; one central concept, however, survived all the changes his approach to literature passed through: his firm Platonic, or Romantic, belief in the enduring nature of the values created by art. He thought this concept of his was confirmed by Wilhelm Dilthey's *Geistesgeschichte*, his first encounter with which was a heady experience: 'It made language again my most important experience, language that now lifted things from the chaotic world of *Werden* into the immobile sky of the fixed stars of *Sein*'.[16] Later his approach was refined by his interest in psychoanalysis (Freud and Jung), in comparative religion (Rudolf Otto), and mythology (Karl Kerényi), and eventually in Oswald Spengler's cultural morphology.[17]

As previously mentioned, Antal Szerb was associated with the literary and critical journal *Nyugat*. He contributed poetry, short stories, and critical essays to *Nyugat* from 1921 until it ceased publication in 1941, and, although most of the leading journals of the period carried writings by Szerb, it was the forum of *Nyugat* that defined his public image as a modernist critic and writer of originality whose dedication to experimentation produced a unique medium which was the simultaneous expression of his scholarly and poetic gifts. His distinctive stance among the leading critics of his generation was due to the fact that, although the emergence of Modernism has been attributed among other things to the stimulus received by Hungarian poetry from the 'West', Hungarian Modernism was primarily rooted in German and French experiences; this explains the fact that 'information on new trends and works in English and American literatures was as a rule outdated and superficial'.[18] Szerb was the only Hungarian critic who had direct contacts with Great Britain: thanks to a research scholarship he spent a year in London in 1929, and when he returned to Budapest he published a short survey of English literature, *Az angol irodalom kistükre* [A Brief Survey of English Literature], which already shows a most intimate familiarity with English culture. His sense of affinity with some aspects of the mind and sensibility he believed he had discovered in the great works of the literary traditions of England was indeed so strong that time and again he used the language of English poetry for self-definition. When, for instance, he described the thrill of the moment which gave him a sudden insight into the nature of modern poetry at the age of seventeen he said:

> The moment [...] was so beautiful that, being now deeply moved by its memory, I cannot but give a quotation to describe it, but it comes from the greatest of poets, Keats, who when he first read Homer compared himself to Cortez's soldiers when they first glimpsed the Pacific Ocean:
>
> > *And all his men*
> > *Look'd at each other with a wild surmise —*
> > *Silent, upon a peak in Darien.*[19]

Although he published three literary surveys, probably the most adequate medium for his critical mind was the essay. The critics of his generation affiliated to *Nyugat* were labelled the 'essayist generation', because they found in the essay the most appropriate form of expression for their composite aim. Dissatisfied with the spiritual aridity of the positivist literary scholarship dominant at the turn of the century, they thought the essay was the form which could revitalize discourse on art by its reliance on poetic effects. Szerb's own concept of criticism was shaped by nineteenth-century English aestheticism in general and Walter Pater and Oscar Wilde's concept of the critic as artist in particular. His attitude to the essay was somewhat redefined by György Lukács, a regular contributor to *Nyugat* from its beginnings until his Marxist turn in 1918, who, in his early essay on the essay, 'Az esszé lényegéről és formájáról' [On the Essence and Form of the Essay] in 1910 defines the essay as an artistic form that mediates between art and philosophy.[20] The essay as a form, relying on the artistic representation of data coming directly from life, i.e. the work of art it is concerned with, expresses a vision of life as *experience* without it being grounded in conceptual thought, in systematic philosophy: 'The essay is a judgment, but the essential, the value-determining thing about it is not the verdict (as is the case with the system) but the process of judging'.[21]

Szerb's spontaneous and deliberate adoption of this heterogeneous inheritance, Oscar Wilde and Lukács side by side, explains two characteristic aspects of his attitude as a critic: the use of an intensely personal voice to articulate the intuitions of the inspired reader on the one hand, and the search for forms of beauty revelatory of eternal truths on the other.

There is, however, another side to his character as critic. He was averse to submitting to any kind of closed intellectual system; he had a chameleon-like aptitude to adopt, and adapt to, the great systems of thought that emerged during his career to meet his own intellectual needs, yet without ever letting himself be confined by them. In the autobiographical essay quoted above he ascribes his change of attitude to literature that came with maturity when he discovered the new novel after the First World War. He compares the spontaneous language of the new novel, dictated by the free association of ideas, to the style of:

> The Renaissance dancer commended by Castiglione for his trick of dropping his gown again and again as he dances to show that he does not care at all. Heavy weights can be lifted with the gesture of the acrobat, but it is more elegant to pretend that you are picking up a lady's handkerchief. Many things can be conveyed in a conjunction, in an unexpected turn of phrase an avenue can open up to the infinite, *to see the world in a grain of sand...* this is our mission, the mission of the Westernizers, to remove the dignified and outdated stiff collar of Hungarian scholarship and teach it to wear a colourful soft shirt instead. I am neo-frivolous, I said then in pride and sectarian spirit, and in secret I took my frivolity as seriously as Geistesgeschichte.[22]

Szerb scholars have explained the term 'neo-frivolity' in various ways. It has been attributed to the simultaneous presence in Szerb's mind of the writer and the critic: the temperament of an artist wrestling with his own creative problems surfaces in the academic essays and redefines their discourse; the dual perspective enhances self-reflection and eventually leads to irony.[23] It has also been suggested that 'frivolity' may be an expression of Szerb's awareness of a Jewish element in his own temperament: in his *History of Hungarian Literature* Szerb dwells on the combination of irony and sentimentality in Heine, which he calls a uniquely Jewish trait.[24] We can also argue that the combination of high-flown seriousness with ironic bathos shows his temperamental affinity with Heine's role model, Byron, and may be traced back to Byron's own ideal story-teller, Sterne, both of whom Szerb admired greatly.

The essays in the present volume, each representing a different facet of his critical intelligence, have been selected to reflect the issues he found most perplexing or challenging as a critic, and also those which most stimulated his mind as a writer. They cluster around the two main periods in the history of literary culture which he found the most intriguing and delightful at the same time: Romanticism, to which his main heroes belonged, and Modernism, against which he must have measured his own achievement as a writer.

'William Blake' was the first critical assessment of Blake in Hungary, written in 1928, at a time when no work by Blake was yet available in translation. It is in this study that Szerb identifies for the first time the Romantics' greatest discovery, one that he would discuss time and again in his critical works: that of the unconscious and the creativity of the human mind. With a thoroughly reliable knowledge of the Blake corpus and a firm grasp of the traditions, esoteric and mainstream, philosophical and theological, that the main literary figures brought on to the stage, Szerb defines the unique character of Blake's vision in an astonishingly profound and well-informed way:

> The painter and mystic's double vision animates and imbues all things with God's presence with incomparably more reality than does philosophical pantheism in the case of German Romanticism or the virtually obligatory nature-worshipping enthusiasm of the English poets of the Wordsworth–Shelley–Swinburne lineage. These, for all their wild enthusiasm, somehow always stand outside of the Great Oneness and their connection with it is that of Yearning — and Yearning always trains the view on what is outside themselves. Blake, on the other hand, in whom there is neither yearning nor impulse, participates in all things purely through his vision, and his relationship to the Universe is not yearning but a human being's compassionate sympathy with the human world.

The other critical writings on Romanticism here take a different approach. They are excerpts from Szerb's panoramic survey of world literature organized around the most outstanding figures of the narrative. Here Szerb aims to create portraits with the living hues and plasticity of characters in drama or fiction. His portrait of Milton suggests that in his reading Milton anticipates the Romantics' metaphysical quest: he is the great Puritan poet who is of the devil's party. Quoting Satan's monologue in Book I, Szerb says: 'The monologue remains, despite all that fall, an eternal hymn to triumphant individualism, and had Milton written nothing but this, it would ensure for him a place in the pantheon of the greatest'. The great poets of the second generation of English Romanticism represent Szerb's triumph as a portrait painter. His 'Byron' 'bestriding life's highest peaks', for all its petty mannerisms and the great egotisms, is a bravura piece of portrait painting which has the conciseness and coherence of a work of art. Its coda justifies the dramatic tension built up in the main body of the text:

> And yet, despite forebodings, he went off and died in a manner appropriate to a man who had always bestridden the mountain peaks, high above the crowd. The great poseur, the superficial dandy was capable of dying for the ideal that a thousand poets, far more serious and whole-hearted than he, proclaimed from behind the safety of their writing desks. His death retrospectively validates and bestows human value and dignity upon all that he wrote.

Szerb's 'Shelley' ('who brings the vivid and restless cavalcade of colour and rhyme into the modern poem') and 'Keats' (when reading the second Hyperion 'we feel as with the later work of Hölderlin: in his "intensity" the poet is speaking of truths that are beyond the limits of our perception, and we are seized by the *horror sacri*') are engraved deep in Hungarian cultural memory with the sharpness of steel.

'Don Juan's Secret', a sketch rather than a carefully argued essay, shows how in no time Szerb can create an extensive panorama to present the ever-changing concept of love, from the chivalric to the Romantic to the cynic, in which Byron is situated somewhere in the middle of the stage. It gives a good insight into the treatment of love in his various literary works, for example in *The Pendragon Legend* with its pull towards the chivalric, the romantic, and the ironic.

'Rousseau', extracted from one of his major studies, *Hungarian Pre-romanticism* published in 1929, is an example of Szerb's creative adaptation of Freud's theory of the opposite pull of the death instinct and Eros, the twin motors of the human psyche. He made full artistic use of this concept in *Journey by Moonlight* with the hero undergoing a quest for the self through a memory of teenage fascination with self-abandonment in the form of love and death, though ending in the triumph of civilization with the prospect of an unending rite of mourning to come. In Rousseau's obsessive self-analysis and condemnation of civilization Szerb detects the influence of Pietism, but also the articulation of the instinct for self-abandonment in the form of a longing for pre-individual existence and self-annihilation, which anticipate the Romantics' exploration of the abyss of the human soul:

> Life is a continuous effort to stay alive, the willpower to overcome the physical laws of nature; and within heroic humanity's own self resides that greatest enemy, that other desire, that hydra whose self-renewing head needs to be struck off every day.

It is probably no exaggeration to say that most of Szerb's writings on Modernism were stimulated by the aesthetic theses of the early Lukács. One of the most ambitious essays of the *Soul and Form* collection is a study of Stefan George originally published in *Nyugat* in 1908.[25] Lukács's George is a poet of *impassibilité* who creates out of his own being the self-contained form in which his vision of life, distilled entirely from empirical data, can be conveyed: the tragedies he describes are those of the Platonic ideal, 'free from all empirical reality'.[26] On the whole Szerb accepts Lukács's Platonic point of view, but in his own essay he creates a much more extensive panorama of the history of the European mind defined by the great changes in the religious outlook of the various periods of history. George's poetry is seen by him as a combination of Catholic Christianity and pagan antiquity: 'He is the first German poet since the Reformation whose work is not contingent on Lutheranism and its more distant descendants, Romanticism and German philosophy'. Protestant individualism, Szerb claims, has separated the individual from the Cosmic Hierarchy, and interest in the self has eventually led to isolation and alienation. George's greatness as a poet is ascribed to his return to the concept of the microcosm as part of the macrocosm: the self-contained form of his poetry is the reflection of that cosmic order.

Szerb's essay on Henrik Ibsen shows that, however obstinately he sought immanent and everlasting patterns in literature, Szerb was aware of the problem of change. He singles out two problems as organizing principles in Ibsen's plays: the idea of liberty and the use of symbols. In both these matters Szerb suggests that the exhilarating novelty of Ibsen has faded by now. Szerb attributes this change in the reaction to Ibsen to the devastating historical experiences, the effects of the war and the revolutions that changed the sensibility of his generation:

> What gripped young people, us young people, was undoubtedly Ibsen's principal message: freedom [...] but after all our wars and revolutions there is no word that sticks more awkwardly in our throat, none that has been more abused, none that any man with a shred of decency employs with greater circumspection.

Symbols have also lost their intriguing nature; they, however, immediately regain their lustre as soon as we can see them in their concrete, literal meanings as

images that are the products of disturbed minds recently identified as such by
psychoanalytical studies:

> His symbols sometimes reveal sudden, ineffable spiritual depths, sending a
> momentary shudder of self-recognition through us, when we thought that
> what we were watching was an allegory or a pathological case. Now and then
> a sentence seems to come crashing down through several storeys and ends up
> coming to rest in the depths of our soul.

Szerb's several writings on the novel after the First World War add up to a clearly
defined theory of the novel which he discusses in the introduction to the collection
Hétköznapok és csodák [The Everyday and the Miraculous] published in 1935.[27] He
mentions two recent critical theories that in his judgement contributed to a better
understanding of what is going on in the modern novel: Lukács's *Die Theorie des
Romans* (1916), and the researches in classical philology and mythology of the
Hungarian scholar, Károly Kerényi. Szerb embraces Lukács's thesis that the heroic
epic and the novel are the two major forms of the great epic tradition in literature,
the heroic epic reflecting a world where the gods are immanently present, while
the novel reflects a god-forsaken society where the gods are not organically present
in the cosmos but merely the target of a transcendent longing. He also adopts
Kerényi's theses which claim that the ancient Greek novel, built on motives of death
and regeneration, emerged from the religious cults of late antiquity as popularizing
forms of mystery religions.[28] Szerb's own starting point is provided by his view that
'the history of our civilization is a collective tragedy', and he reads the modern novel
as an attempt to save that civilization from final defeat.[29] *Hétköznapok és csodák* can
be read as a prophecy: '(not unlike Lukács) Szerb delineates the outlines of a "new
world": with the apocalyptic zeal and in the enthusiastic tone of prophetic discourse
he inaugurates a cultural-spiritual regeneration'.[30] In the modern novel he detects
the return of the myth, which in Kerényi's view discloses psychic realities, and
suggests that the power of myth will save — or at least humanize — our civilization.

The general trend that in Szerb's view characterizes the modernist novel is a
turning away from the grave social issues and the facts of external reality investi-
gated in terms of everyday events by the nineteenth-century realists and the
exploration of mental and psychic reality which is often conveyed through mythological structures. That deeper reality Szerb considers the 'miraculous'. It is very
interesting to see how his critical interest and judgment are determined by his own
writerly character. A case in point is his excessive admiration for G. K. Chesterton.
Szerb considers Chesterton one of the innovators of the novel form. His essay on
Chesterton, however, is concerned with much more than the crisis of the modern
novel, and is informed by a number of personal motives, Chesterton's conversion
to Catholicism being one of them. In an earlier essay published in *Nyugat* in 1936
Szerb calls Chesterton's conversion 'the greatest paradox of his life' and claims that
in Catholicism Chesterton found the combination of order and the irrational that
he had always sought. After centuries of rationalizing the world:

> Only one great formula is still available in which absolute irrationalism and
> absolute order encounter one another, and that is Catholicism, whose concept
> of order is antecedent to man's attempt to infuse rational order into everything:

> it still has the magic and it is still symbolic because it springs from more ancient
> impressions of the world, a deeper and more inexplicable experience of order
> than the parvenu straightness of the lines of rationalism.[31]

Szerb's *Diary* reveals that in his adolescence and early youth, Catholicism fulfilled a
deep emotional and intellectual need in him: as a student he seriously contemplated
entering a religious order. Furthermore, in Szerb's view Chesterton combined
the virtues of the scholar and the writer of fiction, which enabled him to find a
most sophisticated way to redeem the novel: 'he treated the traditional adventure
and detective story, the thriller, in a manner suitable for the promulgation of his
worldview and the expression of his artistic persona'. This is the form Szerb himself
also experimented with in his own fiction.

Much of *Hétköznapok és csodák* is concerned with new British and Irish fiction.
The most significant experiments are discussed under a separate heading, 'The
Stream of Consciousness Novel and Playfulness', and indeed it is in this type of
novel, with its psychological subtlety and treatment of time, that Szerb finds the
'miraculous', the quality that is going to redeem the novel. Although he defines
Ulysses as the novel of the stream of consciousness par excellence, he considers it a
failure:

> Joyce went as far as possible in his reaction against the external, rational
> representation of the world. He excluded the rational completely from his
> worldview. A world, however, from which reason is entirely absent, is no longer
> a world, or at least it is not the human world.[32]

Virginia Woolf, on the other hand, is seen as the greatest master of this new type
of novel:

> Like *Ulysses*, Virginia Woolf's masterpiece, *Mrs Dalloway*, is also the history of a
> day seen through the mind of a single person. But Mrs Dalloway is not a dimwit
> like Bloom, and she is not interested in metabolism at all. She is an attractive
> and multi-layered personality, with a beautiful life behind her; the reader finds
> it delightful to follow her stream of consciousness as it runs between its two
> flowery banks. In this novel the artistic aim of both the stream of consciousness
> novel and the new concept of time is fully realized: a single day, or indeed a
> single moment, can contain all. [...] When Mrs Dalloway goes to bed in the
> evening we have got to know her entire life from just a single day.[33]

Two novelists stand out from the concise presentation of main characters in the
panoramic view of the European novel after the First World War: Marcel Proust
and Thomas Mann. Both are discussed in a category of their own and both are
seen as novelists who have been able to restore the epic totality to the novel that
was, in Lukács's view, the distinctive feature of the heroic epic. Szerb claims: 'Our
knowledge of the soul has been acquired primarily through literature and, above
all, through the novel. One of the most significant and glorious milestones on the
path of this development is the *oeuvre* of Marcel Proust'. Proust's most significant
innovative move is the rejection of the traditional epic concept of time and the
redefinition of the temporal as a subjective experience as proposed by Bergson's
durée. This resulted in a radical redefinition of consciousness, of memory, and a
suspension of the division between the conscious and the unconscious processes of

the mind:

> A sensibility such as this comes our way perhaps once in a century, if at all.
> He truly fulfilled the desire of Novalis: he dreamt awake and was awake
> in his dreams; things conscious and unconscious achieved unity in him,
> interpenetrating each other.

It is easy enough to see that Antal Szerb considered Thomas Mann the most
significant writer, whose novels he read as subtle responses to the crisis of the novel
as well as the crisis of European civilization. In his assessment of Mann's career up
to the publication of the first two volumes of the tetralogy, *Joseph and his Brothers*,
with the focus on *The Magic Mountain*, Szerb's unqualified enthusiasm for Mann's
art is revealed:

> The magnificence of the formal artistry, the power of the portrayals cannot be
> expressed in the language of the literary historian trained to write simply and
> straightforwardly. It would be necessary to compose a panegyric of the kind
> with which the humanists of old expressed appreciation for each other's work.

Mann's superb achievement is partly explained by his rediscovery of myth as a form
of knowledge deeper than what any other form of intellection can provide:

> Myth is not, as the Enlightenment thought, a poetic artifice or, as the history
> of religion taught, a priestly fabrication, nor even the expression of some
> immemorial need of the human spirit, but something more: one of the most
> splendid embodiments of perception. There are facts concerning the world
> apprehensible only in the form of myth. Ages with no mythology of their own
> are impoverished ages, as they lack knowledge of these truths.

While celebrating Mann's return to myth and his ability to combine the
mythological traditions with the insights of modern psychoanalysis, Szerb seems
to be aware of the dilemmas faced by Mann, who lived in exile at the time and
watched with growing anxiety the way German ideologists tried to appropriate
mythology for the purposes of Nazi propaganda. Mann's correspondence with Karl
Kerényi from the period between January 1934 and June 1955 is one of the most
interesting and moving documents of the response of these intellectuals to Europe's
moral and intellectual crisis. In 1941, while working on the fourth volume of the
Joseph tetralogy, Mann explains in one of his letters to Kerényi his determination
to reclaim mythology from the National Socialists and to use it to express the
humanistic values he thought so important to preserve in those years of darkness.
Referring to the way he modernized mythology by grounding it in the insights
of modern psychology, Mann says: 'I have long been a passionate adherent of this
combination, for actually psychology is the means whereby myth may be wrested
from the hands of the Fascist obscurantists to be "transmuted" for humane ends'.[34]

It seems to be almost telepathic the way that Szerb, in his discussion of Thomas
Mann in 1935, lays special emphasis on the humanism conveyed by Thomas Mann's
mythology:

> This is humanism not as a feeling but as an attitude to life; in practice it is
> primarily a negative stance: abhorrence of the use of force, of tyranny, of the
> crippling of individuality. This is the humanism of the eighteenth century, of

Voltaire and Goethe. It derives from an awareness of human dignity, and from the intellectual's serenity, tenderness, and horror of fighting, for it rises far, far above the passions that provoke human beings to commit bloody barbarities. It is an ethos that is not rooted in any feeling or religion, but solely and uniquely in the intellect. This intellect-based morality has been from Goethe onwards the greatest pride and achievement of the German spirit, and from this the new German world, with its new uncertainty in ethics and intuitions, has diverged the furthest.

This was as far as Szerb could possibly go to warn his readers of the devastating implications of Nazi ideology in 1943, when he was himself already personally exposed to the anti-Jewish laws of his government, as he publicly put his faith in the kind of humanism he believed Mann represented. Szerb's instincts as artist and critic merged completely with his acutely felt sense of responsibility as a thinker. 'I am embarrassed whenever people tell me I am a historian of literature. I am a writer whose topic has, incidentally, been literature,' he writes in his *Diary* in 1943.[35] As a witness to — and all too soon a victim of — the ascendancy of the power of darkness in his own country, Antal Szerb, the writer whose topic was literature, laid an increasing emphasis on literature's being the most consummate form in which the highest moral aspirations of humanity have been embodied.

Bibliography

HAVASRÉTI, JÓZSEF, *Szerb Antal* (Budapest: Magvető, 2013)

KERÉNYI, KÁROLY, *Die griechisch-orientalische Romanliteratur in religionsgeschichtlicher Beleuchtung* (Tübingen: J. C. B. Mohr (P. Siebeck), 1927)

KING, JEMMA L., 'The Third Tower: Journeys in Italy by Antal Szerb', *New Welsh Review*, 104 (2014), <https://www.newwelshreview.com/article.php?id=799> [accessed 10 June 2016]

KONTLER, LÁSZLÓ, *Millennium in Central Europe: A History of Hungary* (Budapest: Atlantis, 1999)

LUKÁCS, GYÖRGY, *A lélek és a formák* (Budapest: Napvilág Kiadó–Lukács Archívum, 1997)

——*Soul and Form*, trans. by Anna Bostock (Cambridge, MA: MIT, 1974)

MANN, THOMAS, *Mythology and Humanism: The Correspondence of Thomas Mann and Karl Kerényi*, trans. by Alexander Gelley (Ithaca, NY: Cornell University Press, 1975)

POSZLER, GYÖRGY, *Szerb Antal* (Budapest: Akadémiai Kiadó, 1973)

SZERB, ANTAL, 'Chesterton', *Nyugat*, 29 (1936), <http://epa.oszk.hu/00000/00022/00606/19200.htm> [accessed 10 June 2016]

——'Könyvek és ifjúság elégiája', in Antal Szerb, *Gondolatok a könyvtárban* (Budapest: Magvető Könyvkiadó, 1981), pp. 675–88

——*Magyar irodalomtörténet* (Budapest: Magvető, 1972)

——'A mai angol regény' [1933], in Antal Szerb, *Hétköznapok és csodák. Francia, angol, amerikai, német regények a világháború után* (Budapest: Magvető, 2002), pp. 242–52

——*Naplójegyzetek (1914–1943)* (Budapest: Magvető, 2001)

——*Die Suche nach dem Wunder: Umschau und Problematik in der modernen Romanliteratur* (Amsterdam & Leipzig: Pantheon, 1938)

——*Száz vers* (Budapest: Magvető, 1957)

SZILI, JÓZSEF, 'The Uncompromising Standards of Nyugat (1908–1941)', in *History of the Literary Cultures of East-Central Europe*, ed. by Marcel Cornis-Pope and John Neubauer, vol. III: *The Making and Remaking of Literary Institutions* (Amsterdam & Philadelphia, PA: John Benjamins, 2004), pp. 70–79

SZIRTES, GEORGE, 'Fuelled by Anxiety: *Journey by Moonlight* by Szerb, Antal', *Times Literary Supplement*, 1 June 2001

WÁGNER, TIBOR, ed., *Akitől ellopták az időt: Szerb Antal emlékezete* (Budapest: Kráter, 1996)

Notes to the Introduction

1. Quoted in György Poszler, *Szerb Antal* (Budapest: Akadémiai Kiadó, 1973), p. 366.
2. He translated into Hungarian Casanova's *Mémoires* and Huizinga's *The Waning of the Middle Ages*, as well as novels by Somerset Maugham, Stephen Leacock, and P. G. Wodehouse.
3. Antal Szerb, 'Könyvek és ifjúság elégiája', in Antal Szerb, *Gondolatok a könyvtárban* (Budapest: Magvető Könyvkiadó, 1981), pp. 675–88 (p. 675).
4. Tibor Wágner, ed., *Akitől ellopták az időt: Szerb Antal emlékezete* (Budapest: Kráter, 1996), pp. 315–18.
5. József Havasréti, *Szerb Antal* (Budapest: Magvető, 2013)
6. Szerb, 'Könyvek és ifjúság', p. 679.
7. László Kontler, *Millennium in Central Europe: A History of Hungary* (Budapest: Atlantis, 1999), p. 342.
8. Antal Szerb, *Naplójegyzetek (1914–1943)* (Budapest: Magvető, 2001), p. 279.
9. Szerb, 'Könyvek és ifjúság,' p. 676.
10. Ibid..
11. Antal Szerb, *Száz vers* (Budapest: Magvető, 1957), p. 5.
12. Ibid., p. 7. 'But poets establish what remains', 'Remembrance' by Friedrich Hölderlin, in Friedrich Hölderlin, *Hyperion and Selected Poems*, ed. by Eric L. Santer (New York: Continuum, 1990), p. 267.
13. In Hungarian criticism he has been compared recently to Julian Barnes, Paul Auster, Milan Kundera, and Lawrence Norfolk for the combination of sophisticated formal experiments and popular entertainment (Havasréti, p. 672).
14. George Szirtes, 'Fuelled by Anxiety: *Journey by Moonlight* by Antal Szerb', *Times Literary Supplement*, 1 June 2001.
15. Jemma L. King, 'The Third Tower: Journeys in Italy by Antal Szerb', *New Welsh Review*, 104 (2014), <https://www.newwelshreview.com/article.php?id=799> [accessed 10 June 2016].
16. Szerb,'Könyvek és ifjúság,' p. 682.
17. Poszler, p. 5.
18. József Szili, 'The Uncompromising Standards of Nyugat (1908–1941)', in *History of the Literary Cultures of East-Central Europe,* ed. by Marcel Cornis-Pope and John Neubauer, vol. III: *The Making and Remaking of Literary Institutions* (Amsterdam & Philadelphia, PA: John Benjamins, 2004), pp. 70–79 (p. 78).
19. Szerb, 'Könyvek és ifjúság,' pp. 676–77.
20. First published in Hungarian in 1910 in *Nyugat*, reissued in his influential collection of pre-Marxist essays, *A lélek és a formák* [Soul and Form], which was published in German in 1911: *Die Seele und die Formen* (Berlin: Egon Fleischel, 1911).
21. György Lukács, *Soul and Form,* trans. by Anna Bostock (Cambridge, MA: MIT, 1974), p. 18.
22. Szerb, 'Könyvek és ifjúság,' p. 683.
23. Poszler, pp. 134 & 136.
24. This is suggested in a tentative way by Havasréti (p. 133) with a reference to Szerb's definition of Heine's spirit as a combination of 'irony and sentimentalism' in *Magyar irodalomtörténet* (Budapest: Magvető, 1972), p. 339.
25. This was to become one of the most ambitious essays of his collection *A lélek és a formák* (1909) and of *Die Seele und die Formen* (1910).
26. 'a versek [...] a tragédiák platóni ideáit [adják meg] csupán, menten minden csak empirikus valóságtól', György Lukács, *A lélek és a formák* (Budapest: Napvilág Kiadó–Lukács Archívum, 1997), p. 116.
27. This was published in a German translation in 1938 as *Die Suche nach dem Wunder: Umschau und Problematik in der modernen Romanliteratur* (Amsterdam & Leipzig: Pantheon, 1938).

28. See especially his essay *Die griechisch-orientalische Romanliteratur in religionsgeschichtlicher Beleuchtung* (Tübingen: J. C. B. Mohr (P. Siebeck), 1927).
29. Antal Szerb, 'A mai angol regény' [1933], in Antal Szerb, *Hétköznapok és csodák: Francia, angol, amerikai, német regények a világháború után* (Budapest: Magvető, 2002), pp. 242–52 (p. 243).
30. Havasréti, pp. 306–07.
31. Antal Szerb, 'Chesterton', *Nyugat*, 29 (1936), <http://epa.oszk.hu/00000/00022/00606/19200.htm> [accessed 10 June 2016].
32. Szerb, 'A mai angol regény', p. 574.
33. Ibid.
34. Thomas Mann, *Mythology and Humanism: The Correspondence of Thomas Mann and Karl Kerényi*, trans. by Alexander Gelley. (Ithaca, NY: Cornell University Press, 1975), p. 100.
35. Antal Szerb, *Naplójegyzetek (1914–1943)* (Budapest: Magvető, 2001), p. 280.

PART I

Essays on Romanticism

CHAPTER 1

William Blake (1928)[1]

The English literary world is currently celebrating the centenary of the death of William Blake, the poet, engraver, and mystic. Thanks to substantial tomes and bibliographies as well as articles in the popular press readers have been aware for some time that Blake is one the greatest of English poets and these days he is known as such even beyond the shores of his homeland. However, as little has been written about him in Hungary apart from encyclopedia entries, this centenary offers me an opportunity to make the Hungarian reader at least a little more aware of his significance.

I.

To the poet William Blake everything that happened did so literally. He is a textbook example, a poet *wie er im Buche steht*. Another poet will speak of his inspiration as the feeling that someone or something is dictating what to write, but Blake could put a name to the spirits at whose prompting the endless streams of his prophetic books came rolling out. Another will speak of visions passing before the mind's eye, but whereas he remains aware that those visions are begotten of playful fantasizing, for Blake factual reality is far less real than those visions that conjure the dead to life before his eyes, that reveal to him the secrets of Creation in panoramas that reach to the skies and build for him the Celestial City, a New Jerusalem on the streets of London. Yet another poet will assert that contemporaries do not understand him and that his true greatness will be recognized only a hundred years hence, but for none of them is this so totally the case as for Blake, whose own contemporaries were not even aware that he wrote verse (because had they seen any they would have thought it a novel) and who was referred to only as an engraver in nineteenth-century handbooks, while today, a century on, the dust jackets of popular editions in America proclaim that 'no bookshelf is complete without Blake's poems'.

Of all the many eccentric poets of his eccentric nation Blake was the most eccentric. Everything about him was totally odd. Those interested need to home in on him in a very distinctive atmosphere, as if they were in 'The Crystal Cabinet' of which he wrote:

> Another England there I saw
> Another London with its Tower
> Another Thames & other Hills
> And another pleasant Surrey Bower.[2]

and glimpsed another world, which alone had reality for Blake.

Even how he gained his reputation is a curious story. The books that Blake himself had put together were no longer to be found when, for the first time, one volume was published by a Spiritualist doctor and as a Spiritualist tract.[3] That he was a poet it was only the Pre-Raphaelites that discovered when hunting among the many commonplace poets for oddball forebears of their distinctive mood. It was Dante Gabriel Rossetti who was first led, by some mysterious sympathetic intuition, to the older and perhaps England's first painter-poet. Rossetti was the first to publish Blake's *oeuvre*, as well as the first major Blake biography, by Alexander Gilchrist.[4] The other Rossetti, William Michael, the leading authority on Shelley, added to what was known about him,[5] and Swinburne wrote the first major study of his aesthetics.[6] His complete works were furnished with a commentary by W. B. Yeats, the great Irish visionary poet,[7] and the most entertaining popularizing work about him we owe to G. K. Chesterton.[8] Thus Blake's reputation is inseparably bound up with the outstanding figures of recent English literature.

2.

Blake's biography is a simple man's simple life, interrupted on occasion bizarrely by unforeseen intimate events. Born in London in 1757, into what was, according to Alfred Thomas Story, a fairly prominent but impoverished English family, one of his ancestors was alleged to have been an admiral.[9] Yeats claims to have heard that Blake is of Irish ancestry: for how could anyone who sees visions *not* be of Irish ancestry? His father was a hosier and only in one particular was the peaceful atmosphere of this middle-class family unusual: the entire family were enthusiastic devotees of the teachings of Swedenborg, then only recently translated into English. Had Blake written an autobiography, he would undoubtedly have begun the outset of his intellectual life at the family table of a winter evening, with a cup of tea and Swedenborg's book, when he first started to plumb, word by word, the secrets of heaven and hell. About his physical existence or his bodily birth — before which he deemed he had already lived countless years — or his physical mother, to whom he addressed the following cruel words, he cared little:

> Didst close my Tongue in senseless clay
> And me to Mortal Life betray:
> The Death of Jesus set me free,
> Then what have I to do with thee?[10]

Already as a child he was attended by visions. His wife recounted the first such to Henry Crabb Robinson: '[God] put His head to the window'. He also saw an oak 'filled with angels' and once in a field he encountered the prophet Elisha;[11] but when he related these events at home, his mother gave him a beating and his visions did not return for a long time.[12]

And now art got him in its thrall, art for art's sake, without any visionary metaphysical backdrop. He became an assiduous engraver, spending many years learning the craft, sitting on a high chair and drawing in Westminster Abbey, where he imbibed for all his life the magic of Gothic form, which would become the soul of English Romanticism as yet unborn. But once, in a burst of anger (he was renowned for his excitable temper), he pushed a fellow student away from the easel and young painters were thenceforth banned from the Abbey.

Love, too, paid him a call, first in the form of the False Maiden, then in the shape of the Consoler. He later made an honest woman of this consoling soul, Catherine Boucher by name, and as his wife she was his helpmeet and friend, and served him with a martyr's devotion all his life. 'She was the hardworking burden-bearer to her industrious husband', writes his friend and first biographer, the sculptor and painter Frederick Tatham, from whom we also know that the poor woman's lot was not of the easiest.[13] Blake was quite unconcerned about any worldly matter; he could not be asked for money, and if Mrs Blake ran out of earthly necessities, she resorted to gazing mournfully at her husband until he grasped what was the matter. When she married Blake she could not even write. Subsequently she blossomed to such a degree that she became an assistant to her husband in his drawing; and not only did she believe every word of his visions, but she too learnt the art of having them. Whenever Blake's visions deserted him, they would spend whole nights on their knees, praying together for their return.

As a married man, Blake buckled down to his job as breadwinner. For him this was copperplate engraving, pursued to the end of his days, amidst visions and sublimities, but to the last with the master craftsman's sober and unconditional love for his work. In his time he was famed as a book illustrator: he illustrated Edward Young's *Night Thoughts*, Robert Blair's *The Grave*, and editions of Virgil and Dante. Most prized by connoisseurs is the atmosphere both monumentally sombre and abounding in genuine Blakean idiosyncrasies of his illustrations to *The Book of Job*. He was the first ever to illustrate Chaucer's *Canterbury Tales*, an idea plagiarized by a publisher, unleashing a pamphlet war to the polemics of which we owe Blake's verbal, non-allegorical statements on art in the *Descriptive Catalogue*.[14]

3.

Blake the artist is just as unique a phenomenon as Blake the poet, as every manifestation of both forms shared the same root. Just as certain images recur obsessively in his poems, so do stereotypical forms keep reappearing in his pictures: the Blakean Old Man, with what Chesterton calls his 'snowstorm' of a beard and representing sometimes Death, sometimes God, but mainly the Ancient of Days, a figure in Blake's mythology; the monster with a little green proboscis, which always calls to mind the Freudian explanation with regard to the snake: an angst-ridden phallus; then the spirits, which always descend head first, but express wonderfully and with remarkable clarity the entire paradoxical nature of Blake. Again in Chesterton's words: Blake's supernaturalism 'was the only natural supernaturalism'.[15]

But it is in his drawing technique itself that the greatest paradox is evident. Blake, a man whose experience was of the most obscure secrets of life and the most inexpressible intuitions, found anything lacking firm and definite contours repugnant. As an artist he was strictly linear; he hated oil painting 'because no definite line, no positive end to the form could, even with the greatest of his ingenuity, be obtained: all his lines dwindled and his clearness melted'.[16] He

abhorred Rubens and Titian, and especially their later English disciple Joshua
Reynolds, and — more than half a century before the Pre-Raphaelites — urged a
return to the linear art of Raphael and his predecessors. For him the battle between
the possibilities of linear and painterly style, extending far beyond the limits of art,
towered into a gigantomachy of metaphysical principles.

The art of the line is the true vision, all else is falsehood, merely the work of
the God of this World; it is not eternal. 'The Infinite alone resides in Definite &
Determinate Identity', he says:[17]

> [...] he who wishes to see a Vision; a perfect Whole,
> Must see it in its Minute Particulars; Organized & not as thou
> O Fiend of Righteousness pretendest; thine is a Disorganized
> And snowy cloud: brooder of tempests & destructive War.[18]

The strict ethics of this stance of Blake's in support of firm lines, in both drawing
and in his vision of life, marks him out as a classicist and sets him apart from
German Romanticism, with which in other respects he shows so much kinship.
As Helene Richter rightly points out: 'Because, unlike the German Romantics, for
whom mystery was represented by the Blue Flower and who revelled in vague and
uncertain intimations and longings that they considered the ideal state of the soul,
Blake identified mystery with the Fall and the great curse, and what he sought was
the sunlit clarity of the secrets in the depths of the chasm.'[19]

And this is why Chesterton, the Catholic, asserts that Blake, despite all his
aberrations, is on the side of the angels. While eastern mysticism of the devilish
kind dissolves individuality and conflates it with the universe, western, angelic
mysticism respects the straight line and the distinctive world of each individual.

4.

Though in his time he was known only as an engraver, Blake himself regarded
his poetic calling as more significant. His first collection, *The Poetical Sketches*,
was published in 1783 by his amateur friends, with a pious preface by one Rev.
Mr. Mathews vindicating Blake's brilliant eccentricities and presaging a great, if
conventional, future for the young poet. This is, in fact, Blake's only work that is
not eccentric: it contains poems intended to be no more than poems of lyrical self-
expression. At this time the prophetic pose was quite alien to him, but in terms of
poetic technique he already differed from all his predecessors and Yeats considers
this the first collection of Romantic verse. In it Blake was inspired by forerunners
that his contemporaries were as yet little aware of: the archaic strophes of Edmund
Spenser, the Elizabethan lyric with its inexhaustible wealth of feeling. Through the
medium of his fragmentary *King Edward the Third* Blake was the first to bring to
light the treasure hoard of the Elizabethan drama, hitherto buried far from view.
To the genuine, unique strains of the English lyre, those of Shakespeare, Spenser
and Milton, which had seemed lost for centuries, the lifeless 'diction' of French
Classicism having killed off all lyrical vibrancy, and in which Wordsworth and
Shelley were later to ring out the choicest stanzas of English poetry, Blake was the
first to find his way home.

In Blake all the strands of pre-Romantic art come together. During those youthful years still only the most outwardly aspect is noticeable: his turning towards the past. Blake, too, absorbs those bibles of pre-Romanticism: Ossian, Chatterton's forgeries, Percy's Ballads; in Westminster Abbey he learns that 'Mathematic Form is Eternal in the Reasoning Memory. Living Form is Eternal Existence. | Grecian is Mathematic Form | Gothic is Living Form'.[20]

Aside from *The Poetical Sketches* only one of his works appeared in print in his lifetime, the insubstantial *The French Revolution* (1791). The rest of his work discovered for itself that distinctiveness intimately bound up with the atmosphere of Blake's verse and largely contributory to his work remaining unknown. For, after he had suffered for a long time in constant battles with publishers, there appeared to him one night his dead younger brother's spirit, with whom he was in any case in daily contact, and who taught him how to produce his books himself. This made it possible for Blake to engrave both his images and his letters on the same plate, colouring the sheets in later, each individually by hand. According to John Sampson it was his artistic bent that led him to produce his books himself, just as later with William Morris.[21] Those books that he made himself are of course nowadays very rare and extremely valuable.

That is how Blake's first truly characteristic volume of poetry, *The Songs of Innocence*, was produced in 1789. *The Songs of Innocence* were written for and about children. These are light, playful poems, about chimney sweepers, nurses, infants and especially lambs, often displaying a degree of clumsiness and exaggerated naivety that calls to mind Expressionist painters' works informed by the plastic art of Africa. But all the poetry in the volume wears a mask — it is allegorical, if you like — and it makes room for the extreme expression of one of the most intensive formative yearnings of pre-Romanticism, that for Arcadia. The great Rousseauesque escapist longing for nature, primeval simplicity, for true Man; only, whereas generally the yearning for Arcadia sought as its disguise the milieu of 'primitive' peoples, shepherds, or fairy tales, with Blake it is the world of childhood that takes on the role of Arcadia. And whereas in the older Arcadia of Virgil it was the Roman nobility who strolled about in the guise of shepherds and shepherdesses, in Blake it is vast metaphysical concepts that gambol in the meadows disguised as fathers, children, lambs and friendly lions wearing crowns. The children symbolize humanity before the Fall, that is to say, before the awareness of guilt, and show how beautiful life would be if we could rid ourselves of that.

The Songs of Innocence are still normal poems, with stanzas, rhymes, and for the most part with accessible meanings — indeed, with an explicit aim. But in this same year, 1789, he produced his first two 'prophetic' books, *The Book of Thel* and *The Book of Tiriel*. In lengthy, entirely modern, blank free verse, mythical figures from a non-existent mythology parade before us. Their names — Tiriel, Ijim, Har — sound as though sprouted from some apocryphal biblical work, but occasionally there is a Greek-sounding name: Heuxos, Theotormon, Enitharmion, or one with a Romantic Ossianic Celtic ring to it, such as Mnetha or Leutha. The action — if, indeed, such weird, stereotypical, allegory-filled incidents can be termed action — is enacted on measureless cliffs and jungles and dark seas of some Miltonian primeval world; the figures emerge out of one another in a Gnostic-Neo-platonic manner, enchaining each other, dismembering one another, fleeing, committing incest, setting the world ablaze and calling down curses from on high. This is the world of creation myths, and Blakean mythology shows striking similarities to ancient cosmologies that Blake could never have known of. The seer had plumbed again the depths of the mind's more primeval strata, from which once upon a time the astral legends had become detached.

From Blake's earlier prophetic books (such as *The Daughters of Albion, America, The Song of Los, The Book of Abania,* and *The Song of Urizen*) there emanates incomparable poetic quality amidst a welter of images whose plasticity and singular rhythmicality thrill us even if we understand not one jot of their allegorical content. But the later, monumental prophecies (*Vala, or The Four Zoas, Jerusalem, Milton*) are, discounting a few places of startling philosophical depth, unrhythmic, abstract, and unreadable.

The Marriage of Heaven and Hell, which André Gide translated into French, and *The Songs of Experience* are accessible to all. The latter contains shorter poems and, as its title suggests, is a continuation of *The Songs of Innocence,* with often titles, too, identical, as if to show the same things but from another perspective, that of Experience and Guilt. Love, which the children had pursued as an innocent game, now becomes a dark, mysterious sin. *The Marriage of Heaven and Hell* is a riposte to Swedenborg and Blake's most straightforward statement, and in the form of 'memorable visions' defines the propositions of Blake's Satanism, touched on below. Many shorter poems, perhaps his finest, remained in manuscript in the Rossetti and Pickering MSS until discovered by later devotees.

5.

Blake's life passed quietly amidst his poetic and engraving work; he was never short of generous patrons, like William Hayley, the poet and landowner on whose Felpham estates Blake and his wife spent a good three years. It was here that, returning home one evening, Blake discovered a soldier in his garden and threw him out by force, whereupon the soldier took him to court for cheering Napoleon (which he may well have done). The case came to trial but on Hayley's intervention Blake was acquitted. Blake immortalized the soldier as an important evil spirit in one of his prophetic pieces. Later he took a dislike to Hayley, nothing being harder to endure than a good turn, and accused him of nothing less than trying to seduce his wife and hiring an assassin to do away with him.

From Felpham he moved back to London, where a Spiritualist, John Varley, took him under his wing in the hope that the seer would summon up for him the spirits of the dead. Blake indeed proved very obliging and drew on request images of dead English rulers as they appeared to him, sat down at his table, and jostled to be drawn first. He drew *The Man who Built the Pyramids* and *The Ghost of a Flea,* the latter in two versions even, one with mouth closed and the other after opening its mouth while being drawn, so that its long, sharp teeth were revealed. But all those spirits were visible to Blake alone and Varley was not at all happy with the business...[22]

There now ensued Blake's unhappiest years, 1810 to 1817. His biographers can point to no patrons or source of income in this period. Silence on this matter would appear to support Keynes's view, based on an article in the *Revue britannique*, that Blake spent these years in a mental asylum.[23] During this period he did not write, having completed his last prophetic work, *Milton*, in 1810. By this time he had woken up to the fact that there was no need for him to write anything down, as he had discovered a form of communication peculiar to himself with the help of which he transmitted his works as soon as they came into being directly to his most faithful readers, the angels. As he himself stated there were 'six or seven epics as long as those of Homer and twenty tragedies, as long as Macbeth',[24] that enjoyed great success in heaven and were regularly read by the angels. 'I am more famed in Heaven for my works,' he said, 'than I could well conceive. In my Brain are studies & Chambers filld with books & pictures of old which I wrote & painted in ages of Eternity. before my mortal life & whose works are the delight & Study of Archangels. Why then should I be anxious about the riches or fame of mortality'.[25]

Or, as he puts it so wonderfully in one of his poems,

> For above Times troubled Fountains
> On the Great Atlantic Mountains
> In my Golden House on high
> There they Shine Eternally.[26]

He spent his final decade peacefully in London, in the attitude of the prophet in repose, surrounded by his young disciples and acolytes. He was considered insane by his contemporaries, notably Leigh Hunt, who wrote that once when they were out walking Blake suddenly doffed his hat. Leigh Hunt asked whom he was greeting and Blake replied: 'It's nothing. Just that St Paul the Apostle was flying this way'. But his death was like that of a saint, a saintly artist: on his deathbed he made a drawing of his wife and drifted off singing hymns of his own composition. After his death Frederick Tatham, who was a member of the strict millenarian sect, the Irvingites, and as such accorded himself the title of angel, allegedly had Blake's posthumous papers burnt, claiming that they had been inspired by the devil. (His editor John Sampson cast doubt on the bonfire, Yeats thought it was true.)

6.

In writing about him we cannot avoid the leading question of research on Blake: in what did Blake's prophecy actually consist? At that great turning point of an age when centuries-old classical traditions were crumbling in order to give way to the new — by which I mean the age-old — what was the dogma, or rather the approach, which for all its distinctive individualism summed up the whole current of the age in an incomparably pregnant manner? (In Van Tieghem's comprehensive work on pre-Romanticism, no name crops up more frequently than Blake's).[27]

To this question every Blake scholar offers a different answer, because each garners from his reading of Blake's profoundly suggestive prophecies a message all his own. This is unsurprising, as in Blake this new vision still offered a concrete whole and embraced all the new tendencies that later became differentiated and distinct, turning into what we call the nineteenth century. In the work of Blake, as in that of Goethe, this entire complex is present. That is why Swinburne is right to see in him a pantheist, Rossetti to call him a religious Christian artist in the manner of Dürer, Ellis and Yeats to derive from reading his prophecies truths concerning art theory and inspirational art, Pierre Berger and Arthur Symons to seek in him a forerunner of, respectively, Bergson and of Nietzsche,[28] and Helene Richter, too, in trying to understand him in terms of Romanticism's schizoid view of the self.[29] All of this is present in Blake, and he is thus the forerunner of everyone from Wordsworth to Whitman, from Schelling to Freud.

Undoubtedly, however, it is the experience of mysticism that provides this endlessly complex content with its vital core. Blake falls within the wave of mysticism that engulfs the eighteenth century and undergirds the structures of rationalism and the Enlightenment, with as its two opposing poles Swedenborg, the pure seer, and the magician Cagliostro, and represented in England by Wesley and Methodism.[30] Blake's first intellectual experience was Swedenborg at the tea table, later reinforced by that great powerhouse of Romantic mysticism, Jacob Boehme, of whose work Novalis said, alluding to his *Aurora*:

> On this book's pages does dawn
> Burst with a vengeance into time.[31]

But these intellectual precursors would matter not a whit had Blake not been acquainted from his earliest days with the experience of mysticism, the *unio mystica*, that awareness of being at one with God and the universe, which Swinburne regarded as pantheism:

> [...] but he kissed me and wishd me health.
> And I became One Man with him arising in my strength:
> Twas too late now to recede. Los had enterd into my soul:
> His terrors now posses'd me whole! I arose in fury & strength.[32]

This is union with the highest powers and this awareness of them colours Blake's distinctive sensibility. This is a mysterious mystic union in which every object experiences its own essence, and thereafter the real world does not reside outside but within, all else being but illusion. Blake, too, subscribes to this eternal mystic tenet:

> [...] as in your own Bosom you bear your Heaven
> And Earth, & all you behold, tho it appears Without it is Within
> In your Imagination of which this World of Mortality is but a Shadow.[33]

The theology of those lines is an enigmatical theology, in which God Himself, no less, is within us, and prompts the French authority on Blake, Pierre Berger, to think this almost tantamount to saying that Blake has no God.[34] Blake does, however, believe in God, but warns:

> Seek not thy heavenly father then beyond the skies:
> There Chaos dwells & ancient Night.[35]

And elsewhere:

> Thou also dwellst in Eternity
> Thou art a Man God is no more.[36]

Mystics dwell among us and yet inhabit another world — because the affairs of this world, which we believe to possess absolute validity, are for them no more than symbols; the entire world of Phenomena is but an allegory of something else: the Other, the Real. It is in this sense that the Romantic-Symbolist vision of the world has its origins in Blake's mysticism. In Blake, just as in Hölderlin, even the most concrete geographical concepts are but symbols: Europe symbolizes abstract reason and America freedom.

This is what Blake's 'double vision' consists of. The whole world, with which his obsessed soul is so eternally one, stands vis-à-vis himself in a mysterious correspondence, whereby things insignificant for others are for him transformed into deeply meaningful monitions; he understands the language of objects, because he sees through and into them, beyond Illusion to Reality. 'He who does not imagine in stronger and better lineaments, and in stronger and better light, than his perishing and mortal eye can see does not imagine at all',[37] pronounces that painter and mystic, who distilled his very soul into his vision. In a verse letter to Thomas Butts he describes all that had happened to him on his walk: his dead father had come after him, 'hovering upon the wind', followed by his dead younger brother and his elder brother John, 'the evil one', also dead, and hiding 'in a black cloud'. In the end he struck a thistle which had been urging him to stay:

> What to others a trifle appears
> Fills me full of smiles or tears
> For double the vision my Eyes do see
> And a double vision is always with me.
> With my inward Eye 'tis an old Man grey,
> With my outward a Thistle across my way.[38]

And anyone who thinks a thistle is merely a thistle is a lost man in the eyes of this painter and mystic.

The painter and mystic's double vision animates and imbues all things with God's presence with incomparably more reality than does philosophical pantheism in the case of German Romanticism or the virtually obligatory nature-worshipping enthusiasm of the English poets of the Wordsworth-Shelley-Swinburne lineage. These, for all their wild enthusiasm, somehow always stand outside of the Great Oneness and their connection with it is that of Yearning — and Yearning always trains the view on what is outside themselves. Blake, on the other hand, in whom there is neither yearning nor impulse, participates in all things purely through his vision and his relationship to the Universe is not yearning but a human being's compassionate sympathy with the human world.

It was Blake who, even before Dostoevsky, found the finest words to express the mystical feeling that all the pain deep down in things becomes somehow one and is actually that of a Mysterious Oneness. Blake's long, incomparably striking string of 'proverbs' provides constant variations on this theme;[39] this is the message of the puzzling ballad *The Grey Monk*:

> For a Tear is an Intellectual Thing
> And a Sigh is the Sword of an Angel King
> And the bitter groan of the Martyrs woe
> Is an Arrow from the Almighties Bow.[40]

His double vision is perhaps what differentiates Blake most clearly from other mystics and defines his distinctive place in the history of literature and mysticism. Shelley and Swinburne were 'merely' poets, not mystic seers, while Swedenborg was only a mystic and not a poet. However, even if poet mystics ever existed in the centuries of mysticism, none of them contained in their person a painter also. Other poets tried to put into words the feelings involved in mystical experience, but none had Blake's ability to depict its content, its visions and, above all, the visible world as a seer's vision transformed by his mystic imagination. 'The other [mystics] drew their symbols from theology and alchemy, and he from the flowers of spring and the leaves of summer.'[41]

7.

Nowhere do the idiosyncratic colours of that mystic vision of Blake's, lit as it is by an intense, subterranean glow, shine forth so brightly as when he is professing his ethical convictions; they, too, in their hyperbole form to a certain extent a distinctive chapter in the history of mysticism.

All mysticism is a revolt. The mystic, turned in on his own secret, exclusively internal experiences, disdains all that is external, all that the common run of mortals regard as important, great, even sacred. St Bernard with his blazing zeal, Thomas à Kempis with his apodictic stillness castigate the vanities of human perception. Meister Eckhart and German mysticism out of which sprang Luther's 'sola fides justificat' — faith alone brings salvation — declare human deeds and good works supererogatory: 'General Good is the plea of the scoundrel, hypocrite & flatterer',[42] proclaims Blake. Actions are regulated by laws, while every mystic holds himself to be above the Law. Laws apply only to those who are not elect, not redeemed, and they who seek salvation by obeying rules are misguided, as all mysticism teaches that those alone find salvation who disobey the rules as a consequence of their experience of the redeemed condition.

This is where Blake's mysticism meets the emergent nineteenth century and, like German Romanticism, flows into the new century's wider stream of thought, Liberty. The currents of mysticism and rationalism alike are fed by this stream, and the shackles worn for millennia, or perhaps even from eternity, now begin to bite into and wound the human soul. Blake is one of those who cry out in the greatest pain.

Blake's basic ethical stance is that of the Rebel. In the dark fantasies of his Satanic bitterness he is already suggestive of Baudelaire and his circle, pointing far beyond the optimistic rebels of the beginning of the century. At other times, when depicting the universal bondage of his age, he could almost be taken for one of the most modern poets, in their collective distress:

> Every house a den, every man bound: the shadows are filld
> With spectres, and the windows wove over with curses of iron:
> Over the doors Thou shalt not; & over the chimneys Fear is written:

> With bands of iron round their necks fasten'd into the walls
> The citizens: in leaden gyves the inhabitants of suburbs
> Walk heavy: soft and bent are the bones of villagers.[43]

This is the age of the American War of Independence and the French Revolution, of human rights, of political liberty. Blake walks the streets of London in a Jacobite bonnet, writes a heroic poem about America and the French Revolution, and wants to extend human rights to animals.

But the ideal of freedom for the people could not preoccupy the mystic for very long; for political oppression is of such little importance compared to that other, greater oppression that every man feels in his soul: the enchainment that is Guilt. We carry within ourselves an enemy who has inscribed upon our soul's door 'Do not do it', do not do those things that you most desire to do. This enemy is generally called conscience; Blake calls it the Spectre and his entire mythology is constructed upon the battle between the two opposing forces of Man and the world, Spectre and Emanation (Passion, the *élan vital*, imagination, the emotional in general, or something of that sort):

> Each Man is in his Spectres power
> Untill the arrival of that hour,
> When his Humanity awake
> And casts his own Spectre into the Lake.[44]

How did the Spectre come about — the human abstraction divorced from life as lived — and simultaneously sin and guilt, that dreadful curse of self-searching, conscience-haunted humanity? Is it possible that the Creator — Himself Goodness, who created the world good and beautiful — also created sin? That He who made the lamb created the tiger also?[45] Or who was it?

This is the theme that Blake ruminates upon through all the confusion in his prophetic books and, in order to provide an answer, elaborates his immense mythological system. And this mythology (perhaps the last such in the history of the European spirit) bears a distinct resemblance to that of those who first raised the question of the origin of sin: the Gnostics. Whether Blake was aware of these teachings of Bardesanes and Markion is a moot point.[46] If he was, it could have been only thanks to Mosheim's *Ketzergeschichte*;[47] Pierre Berger is of the opinion that he could not have known this work, while Helene Richter suggests that he did, though she cannot prove it. For centuries a Gnostic tradition has coursed its subterranean way through Europe, surfacing in the Albigensians and perhaps some of the more obscure Reformation sects. Who knows whether this reached Blake by some strange, underground route, or if he arrived by himself at the same conclusions as did the Gnostics some seventeen centuries earlier?

According to the teachings of the Marcionites, the Old Testament Jehovah who created the world and handed down the stone tablets of the Law is not that God who, in His infinite goodness, sent Christ to redeem the world, but a rebellious evil spirit, a demiurge, an artisan, who in his infinite boredom, cast out of primeval unity into the void, created the world, the law, and humankind. The True God has left him and his laws far behind. Those who have gnosis, the perception of the True God, are no longer subject to Jehovah's laws.

Blake's cosmogony is remarkably similar. The world was created by Urizen when his Emanation left him and his Spectral Part remained. He forged chains out of the hours and minutes and bound the world with the fetters of Time and created the Laws. Throughout the immeasurable complexities of the prophetic books Urizen is at war with the blazing, free spirit Los, until with the end of time freedom will prevail and the graves will be opened:

> And milk & blood and glandous wine
> In rivers rush & shout & dance,
> On mountain, dale and plain.[48]

Here we can already see the emergence of the Hegelian rhythmicality of history in that favourite topos of Romanticism, the triad of the world before, during, and after the Fall.

Thus it was Urizen, the evil God, who created the laws; and sin exists only because laws exist. But the mystic, who has discerned Urizen's perfidies and knows that 'Moses beheld upon Mount Sinai forms of dark delusion',[49] has progressed beyond Good and Evil:

> I care not whether a man is God or Evil; all that I care
> Is whether he is a Wise Man or a Fool. Go! put off Holiness
> And put on Intellect.[50]

(by 'Intellect' he does not, of course, mean 'rational thought' but mystic perception).

Everything that appears to be sin is merely a state that the soul passes through but which does not alter its essence. 'Every Harlot was once a Virgin: every Criminal an Infant Love!', and its subsequent transformations are transient states.[51]

Many another mystic has reached this point in his teaching, but what now followed, Blake's *Satanism*, is peculiarly his own, and is bound to be in some correlation with the distinctive architecture of his soul.

If the God of this world and of the Bible is evil, then his servants, the angels, are also evil and it is his enemies, the devils, who are good and true spirits. This distinction was very important to Blake, since he was in daily intercourse with devils and angels, as the arresting visions of *The Marriage of Heaven and Hell* make clear. The angels that put in an appearance here are indeed extraordinarily disagreeable: their law-abiding petty bourgeois philistinism being even accompanied by an element of smug bumptiousness; it is no wonder that Blake's artistic soul could not abide them.

'I have always found that Angels have the vanity to speak of themselves as the only wise; this they do with a confident insolence sprouting from systematic reasoning.'[52] The angels, like all philistines, are rationalists. But they are not incorrigible: Blake succeeded in converting one angel to his own truth. 'This Angel, who is now become a Devil, is my particular friend: we often read the Bible together in its infernal or diabolical sense which the world shall have if they behave well.'[53]

This fateful relationship between angels and devils contributes considerably to Blake's incomprehensibility; it is this reversal of roles that causes him, in Chesterton's words, to 'write one of his most colossal convictions and the average reader thinks it is a misprint.'[54]

All this may seem like whimsy and eccentricity in the eyes of anyone not used, unlike Blake, to debating with angels and dining with prophets. But those contorted, baroque notions had their deep-rooted psychological basis, just as every notion is but a groping in the dark after the curious twists and turns of psychical experience. One of Blake's seemingly cryptic utterances, so far overlooked by his commentators, offers an explanation for his Satanism: 'When Thought is closed in Caves. Then love shall shew its root in deepest Hell'.[55]

When the fettered moral world groans under the weight of guilt, genuine love, primeval Eros, is pronounced a sin — and that is why Blake sides with Hell, with Eros, and opposes the angels. Love is the point where his attack on the Laws and on Guilt is at its most vehement. And by a curious paradox, Blake the mystic becomes an apostle of free love. The whole of *The Songs of Experience* is a paean to this notion, but throughout Blake's *oeuvre*, Freedom is to be understood primarily as the freedom of Love.

Nowhere has any elite been more preoccupied with the notion of free love than in England — perhaps because nowhere is sexual morality so rigid. Blake's younger contemporary, William Godwin (1756–1836), laid the theoretical foundations of free love while his daughter put theory into practice in Switzerland with Shelley, in a *ménage à trois* that aroused feverish interest and outrage among the English public.[56] These, however, were 'freethinkers'; but how did the pious Blake reconcile free love with his religion?

All mysticism is life-affirming. Only superficially is this contradicted by the asceticism practised by the great mystics who mortify their flesh. Asceticism for the mystic is not a goal in itself, certainly not a way of acquiring merit, but merely a means to an end, practical training for the experience of mysticism, the life-affirming rapture of ecstasy. The mystic believes in the boundless sublimity of every moment in life: the moment of ecstasy belongs to our lives and does not stand outside like some world to come, but is rather the highest value of life itself: the mystic basks in sensual joy on this earth and thus cannot wholly repudiate earthly life and its delights. The writings of the great mystics are filled with the expression of sensual pleasure. Mysticism is one variety of Vitalism. 'For every thing that lives is Holy', says Blake.

What is called love is also the framework of ecstatic moments, a mystical experience for those who know how to savour it mystically, and for the ordinary mortal the most straightforward path to ecstasy. In the dream symbolism of psychoanalytic theory the symbols for coitus and ecstasy are identical; it has long been known that mystics and alchemists alike employ coitus — Union — as the symbol of the mystical experience. Thus did Blake's edifice of ideas come to involve free love. The antinomian cult of Liberty and the supremacy of the mystical experience found their culmination in this coalescence.

Blake's biographers claim to know that there was an experiential basis for his anti-marriage period, which lasted from 1790 to 1795. Above all, he wanted to carry out in practice his principle that in love there should be nothing mysterious or hidden; only the guilty and unredeemed have anything to hide from their beloved and it is through this concealment that love turns into sin. His friend John Linnell visited him once and found him and his wife sitting stark naked in the arbour, with *Paradise Lost* in their hands, taking turns to read aloud the words of Adam and Eve in Eden. Linnell was embarrassed and wanted to withdraw but Blake did not let him: '"Come in!"' cried Blake; '"it's only Adam and Eve, you know!"'[57]

His confessional, non-prophetic poetry, which remained in manuscript (such as *In a Myrtle Shade, My Pretty Rose Tree,* or the ballad *William Bond*), show that at one time, irrespective of any theory or prophecy, he had indeed found the 'joyous yoke' of marriage very burdensome:

> Why should I be bound to thee
> O my lovely mirtle tree
> Love free love cannot be bound
> To any tree that grows on ground.[58]

And his yearning to be free of the myrtle tree was not, it seems, entirely impersonal and disinterested. Rossetti already remarks: 'It is known that the shadow of jealousy, far from unfounded, fell on poor Catherine Blake's married life at one moment, and it has been stated that this jealousy culminated in a terrible and difficult crisis'.[59] Ellis and Yeats claim to know more: 'It is said that Blake wished to add a concubine to his household in the Old Testament manner, but gave up the project because it made Mrs Blake cry'.[60] Which could have come as a surprise to no one but Blake himself.

8.

In Blake, as in Dante and in dreams (dream visions and mystical poetry being closely akin), each thing has three layers of meaning. First of all the literal meaning. It is this that Blake scholars, apart from Pierre Berger, are most inclined to neglect. They fail to notice that the endless battles in the prophetic books may be literally battles, those of the primeval forces of nature that created the world. For this is the age of natural philosophy; we are close to the psychic roots of F. X. von Baader, Novalis, and Schelling and even Part II of *Faust* is by now difficult to understand because the natural philosophical speculation which was obvious and literally comprehensible at the time has made it obscure to us. In addition to this meaning it has an emotional meaning or, rather, tendency: the prophetic declaration of rebellion, Liberty, free love. There is also a third level of meaning: the psychological. Pierre Berger, too, regards the mythical creatures as symbolic states of mind.[61] All mystical writing has a psychological objective: Dante's *mistico viaggio* also depicts the journey of the soul within its own realm, through the heights and depths of its own selfhood, until, in the *unio mystica,* it reaches the presence of God seated alone in His own self.

And so Helene Richter is right when she delves into the meaning of those poems about free love and concludes that what they are about is the freeing of the strata of the subconscious, free love being a fragment in concrete form broken off from All Desire slumbering in the vast caverns of the subconscious. Those poems are foot soldiers of the great Romantic revolution which had dug the foundations of poetry one level deeper into the human psyche, releasing and making articulate those levels of the soul until then without a voice, like the barren underworld wastes in Milton's well-known poem.

Those psychological insights, by which I mean Blake's liberation of the sub-conscious, simultaneously caused a revolution in the philosophy of art, the first great feat of arms of Romanticism, in both practice and theory. In practice, because he let his imagination roam unrestrainedly and in his ecstasy is unashamed to haul into his poems those primeval, daemonic forces chained up and sentenced to silence. And as for theory, his poems, both in allegorical disguise but also openly, proclaim that this is what we *must* do. What the French Revolution was to politics, what free love was to society, the mutiny of the Imagination and the revolt of pre-Romanticism and Romanticism was to the realm of poetry.

The first onslaught of pre-Romantic rebellion was directed at rationalism. Blake detested Bacon, the founder of empiricism, because experimentation refers only to the deceptive world of appearances, whereas perception of the real world can be gained only by intuitive means; he detested Newton for mechanizing that interplay of free and vital forces that comprises the universe; he detested the Greeks and also Dryden and Pope, who made poetry Grecian and rational — because 'Mathematic Form is eternal in the Reasoning Memory, Living Form is Eternal Existence | Grecian is Mathematic Form | Gothic is Living Form':[62]

> The Stolen and Perverted Writings of Homer & Ovid: of Plato & Cicero, which all Men ought to contemn: are set up by artifice against the Sublime of the Bible, but when the New Age is at leisure to Pronounce; all will be set right: & those Grand Works of the more ancient & consciously & professedly Inspired Men, will hold their proper rank, & the Daughters of Memory shall become the Daughters of Inspiration.[63]

Inspiration: that second commandment on the stone tablets of pre-Romanticism, the second and decisive charge of the Romantic revolution. For Blake inspiration means more than art; it is a means of bringing works of art into existence. Just as Novalis's circle ascribed to inspired, ecstatic imagination a certain creative power not just artistically but in the objective world (magic idealism), Blake, too, attributes to it a metaphysical role: being inspired means that we have vanquished the Spectre lurking within us, the awareness of sin, which is at the same time abstract, speculative Reason. Man inspired is man redeemed, a happy man, the only truly human being, and the evolution of humanity involves all of us shedding in due course our spectral part and being inspired. For that very reason to be a good Christian is tantamount to being an inspired artist; Christ and the apostles, too, were such.[64] The inspired artist sees right through Appearance to Essence and that insight enables him to take part in the war of the worlds; by means of his art, which depicts Truth, he carries the cause of Truth to victory.

Blake's inspiredness, from the psychological viewpoint, manifested itself above all in his double vision. 'He who does not imagine in stronger and better lineaments, and in stronger and better light than his perishing and mortal eye can see, does not imagine at all. The painter of this work asserts that all his imaginations appear to him infinitely more perfect and minutely organized than any thing seen by his mortal eye.'[65] Blake believes unconditionally in the objective reality of his own vision, as opposed to the rational artist he despises, whose vision is a compilation of memories.

> What seems to Be: Is: To those to whom
> It seems to Be, & is productive of the most dreadful
> Consequences to those to whom it seems to Be.[66]

But Blake's inspiration was not solely visual; he also experienced verbal inspiration and his statements in this respect are much more curious, just as he was generally far closer to the norm as a painter than as a poet. At several points he claimed, with absolute conviction, that he wrote his works at the dictation of spirits, thus with him inspiration appeared on the scene in the extreme form found with the writers of certain holy books, for example — as legend has it — the Septuagint's translators.

> I have written this Poem from immediate Dictation, twelve or sometimes twenty or thirty lines at a time, without Premeditation & even against my Will; the Time it has taken in writing was thus render'd Non Existent, & an immense Poem Exists which seems to be the Labour of a long Life all produc'd without Labour or Study.[67]
> 'I may praise it, since I dare not pretend to be any other than the Secretary; the Authors are in Eternity.'[68]

Thus did Blake realize in the most extreme form the main postulate of the Romantic aesthetic: he was the most 'inspired' poet. Extremes are always at their most extreme at the beginning of movements.

9.

But we cannot resist a little sceptical smile. We wonder what sort of spirits could have dictated to Blake those actually no longer even good poems. Is Chesterton perhaps right in ascribing the poet's later poetical and philosophical faults not to Blake himself but to the fact that he fell in with bad company: all kinds of upstart spirits? What is the psychological explanation for Blake's inspiration?

First of all it might be pointed out that the degree of Blake's inspiredness varied cyclically and increased steadily. He wrote *The Poetical Sketches*, for example, when still at the stage in which all talented poets write their works: his conscious mind still had firm control over his creation. At the time he wrote *The Songs of Innocence* and *The Songs of Experience* and the earlier prophetic books, we believe he had attained the stage achieved only by the extremely great and truly possessed poets, where all the diverse strata of the voluntary and the involuntary, of cogitation and imagination, of the promptings of formal orderliness and the primordial opulence of inner chaos are in total harmony and completely interpenetrate each other: the soul lives the Romantic, joyous time of which Novalis has said 'we are near waking when we dream we are dreaming'. And finally, in the later prophetic books, he exceeds limits never before exceeded by a poet, thus ceasing to be a poet and becoming a *medium*, which does not mean that he literally wrote at spiritual dictation, only that he wrote in a state of mediumnity, switching off his conscious as completely as possible — or, as psychology has it, automatically.

Psychology reckons with several varieties of automatic or medium writing, for which one Helene Smith was particularly famous, as Professor Théodore Flournoy of Geneva University devoted an entire book to her.[69] In her trance-like state Helene Smith composed — or, rather, underwent — two vast novels, one with Marie Antoinette as heroine, the other acted out on the planet Mars. Flournoy had, however, little difficulty proving Blake mistaken, the Daughters of Memory and of Inspiration being identical, given that the entire Marie Antoinette fantasy was based on a novel Smith had read earlier, and the language allegedly spoken on Mars was actually a childish distortion of French. Today we know that nothing, whether in the conscious or the subconscious mind, could not be brought to the surface by memory. Automatic writing, too, consists in the recombining of images stored in the memory, except that here the process of recall takes place entirely unconsciously. Mediumnity is a state of mind whereby elements in the subconscious operate entirely uncensored by the conscious, as happens in dreams. The subconscious element thus endowed with freestanding status is regarded by the medium as a new character. It is that spirit that underlay Blake's inspiration.

Automatic writing may perhaps be seen as the ultimate ideal of the Romantic aesthetic: total spontaneity, the decanting of the hidden Ego into words. The Blakean spectre has finally been 'cast into the lake' and only the Emanation was writing, or, if you will, the soul was emanating.

And yet: examination of the actual contents of automatic writing leads to the opposite conclusion. In automatic writing it is not what is individual that achieves expression, but rather the content that is most general and shared by human beings. Because in this case it is the subconscious that is speaking, and as Jung says, in 'people the subconscious is shared to a far greater degree than the contents of the individual psyche, because the former consists in the distillation of what is the shared average over the longer term.'[70]

We experience that curious sense of surprise even when it is the objective elements, the narrative or the plot of Blake's obscurest works that we are considering. We are amazed to realize that we have met these stereotypical Blakean motifs of incest, ancestral parricide, dismemberment, dragons, and rebirth frequently already. This, as we have said, is the world of cosmogonical myths and these motifs are elements of every people's every creation myth.

How did these myths find their way into Blake's work? For he cannot have known the aboriginal stories of Africa or Australia that match his own, almost word for word. The answer is simple: they reached him from the same place that they reached those ancient creation myths: from the childhood memories stored in the subconscious. In the state of his mediumnity, Blake was thrown back on his subconscious, so he regressed to an infantile state, the infant state of humanity when it gave birth to its creation myths.

More recent folklore research, however, suggests that creation myths are based on the fantasies that play such an important role in every person's childhood, when the child is intent on puzzling out the Grown-Ups' Secret — the mystery of their own birth — and comes up with the most preposterous explanations.[71]

This, then, is the ultimate achievement of Blake's inspiration: when he thinks he is recounting his most distinctive visions, he is in fact sparking off the childhood fantasies shared by all human beings, and the Daughters of Inspiration revert to being the Daughters of Memory. This is a value judgement as well. And yet the Greeks were right after all: the Muses are indeed the Daughters of Memory and there is nothing Romantic about that. The triumph of inspiration is simultaneously its bankruptcy.

But it did not spell bankruptcy for Blake, for he amounted to more than his inspiration: he was a standard-bearer for poets who, when language was renewed by the Romantics, fought on the front line. He was a liberator who gave voice to hitherto unarticulated pain, a mystic pilgrim, who after the lapse of half a millennium stumbled into a world filled with the breath of God and trodden before his time by the Florentine Poet in his Gothic gravity.

Notes to Chapter 1

1. [First published in 1928 (Szeged: Városi Nyomda).]
2. 'The Crystal Cabinet', ll. 9–12 [in *The Complete Poetry & Prose of William Blake*, ed. by David V. Erdman (New York & London: Anchor Books, 1988), pp. 488–89 (hereafter cited as Erdman)].
3. James Garth Wilkinson, ed., *The Songs of Innocence and Experience*. London, 1839.
4. Alexander Gilchrist et al., *Life of William Blake, Pictor Ignotus. With Selections from his Poems and other Writings, recently edited by Dante Gabriel Rossetti*. London and Cambridge, 1863. 2 vols.
5. [Known as the Aldine Edition of Blake, *The Poetical Works of William Blake, Lyrical and Miscellaneous*, ed. by W. M. Rossetti (London: G. Bell & Sons, 1874), with a 130-page introduction by Rossetti.]
6. A. C. Swinburne, *William Blake. A Critical Essay*. London, 1869. Second edition, London, 1906.
7. E. J. Ellis and W. B. Yeats, eds., *The Works of William Blake. Poetic, Symbolic, and Critical*. London, 1893, 3 vols.
8. G. K. Chesterton, *William Blake*. London, n.d. [1910].
9. Alfred Thomas Story, *William Blake*. London, 1893.
10. *To Tirzah*, 13–16 [in Erdman, p. 30].
11. [2 Kings: 2–5]
12. Henry Crabb Robinson in: Gilchrist et al., *Life of William Blake*; I, p. 385.
13. Archibald G. B. Russell, ed., *The Letters of William Blake. Together with a Life by Frederick Tatham*. London, 1906; p. 47.
14. [*A Descriptive Catalogue*, in *The Complete Writings of William Blake*, ed. by Geoffrey Keynes (London: Nonesuch Press, & New York: Random House, 1957), pp. 563–86.]
15. Chesterton, *William Blake*; 7.
16. Tatham, in Russell, ed., *The Letters of William Blake*; p. 11.
17. *Jerusalem*, Ch. 3, Plate 55; 64 [in Erdman, p. 205].
18. Ibid., Ch. 4, Plate 91; 20–23; 833 [in Erdman, p. 251].
19. 'Denn in Gegensatz zu den deutschen Romantiken, denen das Geheimnis die blaue Blume ist, und die in unklaren und unbestimmten Ahnungen und Sehnsüchten als in dem Ideal des Gemützustandes schwelgten, ist für Blake das Mysterium gleichbedeutend mit dem Sündenfalle und dem großen Fluche, und sonnenhelle Klarheit in abgrundtiefen Geheimnissen ist das Ziel, dem er nachstrebt.' Helene Richter, *William Blake*. Straßburg, 1904; p. 110.
20. *On Virgil* [in Erdman, p. 270].
21. John Sampson, ed., *The Poetical Works of William Blake*. Oxford, 1905; XV.
22. John Varley, *A Treatise on Zodiacal Physiognomy*. London, 1828. (Extracts quoted in Arthur Symons, *William Blake*. London, 1907)
23. Geoffrey Keynes, *A Bibliography of William Blake*. New York, 1921; 309. *Revue britannique*, Vol. XIV, July 1833.
24. Henry Crabb Robinson, in: Gilchrist et al., *Life of William Blake*; I, p. 392.
25. [Letter to John Flaxman, 21 September 1800, in Erdman, p. 710.]

26. ['The Caverns of the Grave', ll. 17–20, from Blake's Notebook, in Erdman, pp. 480–81.]
27. Pierre Van Tieghem, *Le préromantisme*. Paris, 1924.
28. Pierre Berger, *William Blake. Mysticisme et poésie*. Paris, 1907; Symons, *William Blake*.
29. Richter, *William Blake*.
30. For the parallels between Blake and Wesley, see Symons, *William Blake*; p. 17.
31. [Translation by Peter Sherwood ('In diesem Buche bricht der Morgen | Gewaltig in die Zeit hinein', 'An Tieck', in Novalis, *Gedichte und Prosa*, ed. by Herbert Uerlings (Düsseldorf: Artemis & Winckler, 2001), p. 111).]
32. *Milton*, Book the First, Plate 22 [24]: 11–14 [in Erdman, p. 117].
33. *Jerusalem*, Ch. 3, Plate 71; 17–19 [in Erdman, p. 225].
34. Berger, *William Blake*, p. 108.
35. *Milton*, Book the First, Plate 20, 32–33 [in Erdman, p. 114].
36. *The Everlasting Gospel*, 70–71 [in Erdman, p. 520].
37. *A Descriptive Catalogue* [in Erdman, p. 541].
38. *With happiness stretchd across the hills....* 25–30 [in a letter to Thomas Butts, 22 November 1802, in Erdman, p. 721].
39. *Proverbs*, in Yeats, ed., *Poems of William Blake*; pp. 96–100.
40. *The Grey Monk*, 29–32 [in Erdman, pp. 489–90].
41. W.B. Yeats, *Preface* in: W.B. Yeats, ed., *The Works of William Blake*. London, 1902; p. 27.
42. *Jerusalem*, Ch. 3, Plate 55: 61 [in Erdman, p. 205].
43. *Europe*, Plate 12, 26–31 [in Erdman, p. 64].
44. *Jerusalem*, Ch. 2, Plate 37, 32–35 [in Erdman, p. 184 and p. 810].
45. [cf. Blake's most famous poem *The Tyger*, in Erdman, pp. 24–25.]
46. [Bardesanes, Syriac theologian, 154–222 CE; Markion, Christian theologian from Sinope, c. 85–c. 165 CE]
47. [Johann Lorenz von Mosheim, *Versuch einer unpartheiischen und gründlichen Ketzergeschichte* (Helmstedt: Christian Friedrich Weygand, 1746).]
48. *The Song of Los*, Plate 7, *Asia* 38–40 [in Erdman, pp. 69–70].
49. *The Song of Los*, Plate 3, *Africa*, 17 [in Erdman, p. 67].
50. *Jerusalem*, Ch. 4, Plate 91, 54–56 [in Erdman, p. 252].
51. *Jerusalem*, Ch. 3, Plate 61, 52 [in Erdman, p. 212].
52. *The Marriage of Heaven and Hell*. Plate 21 [in Erdman, p. 42].
53. *Ibid.*, 192 [in Erdman, p. 44].
54. Chesterton, *William Blake*; p. 143.
55. *Vala, or The Four Zoas*, Plate 65, 12 [in Erdman, p. 344].
56. Blake must have been acquainted with Godwin, since he illustrated one of the works of Godwin's wife, Mary Wollstonecraft.
57. Gilchrist et al., *Life of William Blake*; I. pp. 112–13.
58. *In a Myrtle Shade*, 7–10 [in Erdman, p. 798].
59. Gilchrist et al., *Life of William Blake*; II. p. 87.
60. Ellis and Yeats, eds., *The Works of William Blake*; p. 115.
61. Berger, *William Blake. Mysticisme et poésie*; pp. 144–45.
62. See fn. 20.
63. *Preface to Milton* [in Erdman, p. 95].
64. *A Descriptive Catalogue*, ['The Laocoön', in Erdman, p. 274].
65. *A Descriptive Catalogue* [in Erdman, pp. 541–42].
66. *Jerusalem*, Ch. 2, Plate 36, 51–53 [in Erdman, p. 179].
67. *Letter to Thomas Butts*, 25 April 1803 [in Erdman, pp. 728–29].
68. *Letter to Thomas Butts*, 6 July 1803 [in Erdman, p. 730].
69. Théodore Flournoy, *Des Indes à la planète Mars. Étude sur un cas de somnambulisme avec glossolalie*. Paris, Genève, 1900.
70. '[d]as Unbewußte ist in unendlich viel höherem Grade allen Menschen gemeinsam als der Inhalte des individuallen Bewußtseins; denn es ist die Verdichtung des historisch Durchschnittlichen und Häufigen.' C. G. Jung, 'Wandlungen und Symbole der Libido', in *Jahrbuch für psychoanalytische Forschungen*, Bd. 3/1 (1911), p. 169.

71. See Eduard Stucken, *Astralmythen. Religionsgeschichtliche Untersuchungen*. Leipzig, 1907.

CHAPTER 2

Milton (1941)[1]

His poetry and personality cannot be contained within the bounds of Puritanism: Milton is the great poet of universal Protestantism. From his early youth he lived a life that shunned the everyday, devoting himself initially to poetry, then to his religious and political ideals, with the two eventually entwining in his soul to bring forth *Paradise Lost*. As a young man he prepared for the poet's calling with total conviction, aware from the outset that he would create something that would be an eternal ornament of the spirit. Studying in Italy when the Revolution of the Saints erupted in England, he hurried back to play his part in the wars. He married but the marriage was ill-starred, as his wife could not bear the poet's inhuman gravitas and unrelenting intellectual demands. He composed a vast baroque disquisition, crammed with citations, on the justifiability of divorce, but he failed to learn from his experience and married twice more without surrendering any of his awesome dignitas: even his daughters could not bear to share his house. During the stormy wars of religion his muse fell silent and he become secretary to Cromwell and penned fiery treatises on behalf of the Cause. Only when the Puritans' empire collapsed did he return, broken in body and soul and having lost his eyesight — 'fallen on evil days' — , to the great poetic ambitions of his youth.

The play of poetic imagination in Milton is at its most powerful in the poems of his early years: in *L'Allegro*, which celebrates the pure joys of life, in *Il Penseroso* (1633), a meditation on loneliness and the melancholy of the Baroque, and in his lament *Lycidas* (1637). He also wrote *Comus* (1634), a ceremonial masque.

The great products of his second period, in addition to some sonnets — unforgettable, as if carved in marble — were his tracts. Some of these are today as inaccessible as the other theological tracts and political disputations of the seventeenth century; Taine likens these polemicists to dinosaurs, with their endless, patient argumentation, awkward vulgarity, reams of quotations, and sentences that ramble on for two or three pages. But one of Milton's disquisitions, the *Areopagitica*, has lost little of its force and topicality over the years: it concerns the freedom of the press. It is to its free press, he wrote, that England owes the fact that news of its scholarly achievements has reached the farthest corners of the earth: 'Nor is it for nothing that the grave and frugal Transylvanian sends out yearly from as far as the mountainous borders of Russia and beyond the Hercynian wilderness, not their youth but their staid men, to learn our language and our theologic arts'. If there were no evil in the world, there would be no merit in man's opting for good; evil books must be permitted to circulate freely, so that people might freely choose the good. The state cannot humiliate its citizens by treating them as minors, as Plato wanted.

In his younger days he intended to write an epic about King Arthur but after the great traumas of his adulthood there was only one topic that he deemed worthy, the Holy Writ. *Paradise Lost* begins in the endless wastes of the Underworld where Satan and his coevals are recovering consciousness after their fall: they hold council and resolve on the ruin of mankind. Those in Heaven observe how Satan steals his way across the world towards Paradise; an archangel calls on Adam and Eve to alert them lest they commit sin unawares. By way of warning the archangel retails the fall of the rebellious angels, but in vain. Eve, out of female foolishness, eats of the forbidden fruit while Adam, chivalrous and in love with her, follows suit so that Eve does not have to endure on her own the suffering that awaits. Thus does the woman-despising male pride of Puritanism provide its distinctive version of the Fall.

Unlike the engaging works of Homer and Dante, *Paradise Lost* is not a masterpiece that continues to be relevant today. Milton was too much a man of his time. His work is disproportionately filled with theological argumentation, and his style, though it may at times soar to classical heights, is often prosaic. His imagination, too, is closely wedded to his age. Of course, no one is in a position to say precisely how our ancestors lived in Paradise and the angels in heaven; still, Milton's presentation gives us pause. Let us take the famous scene where the archangel Raphael pays a visit. Eve, the thoughtful English housewife, has prepared a copious vegetarian lunch for him, and as he is refreshing himself with relish she discreetly withdraws and a learned dialogue between the archangel and Adam ensues: both are as grave and uncompromisingly self-important as the Englishmen of that century. Heaven, too, has a distinctly seventeenth-century quality: God is the great plenipotentiary monarch (a Baroque image: the outstanding seventeenth-century Hungarian-Croatian poet Zrínyi also portrays God as a monarch), but one not governing his realm with the approval of all. During a sumptuous court ceremony he crowns Christ as his successor but the jealous ones confer and whisper among themselves. The angelic Estates of the Realm live under military discipline amidst the mighty bastions of heaven, arsenals, and gunpowder stores, just like Cromwell's Ironsides: when Raphael passes before them they present arms. This empire of the empyrean — oh, Baroque century! — is held together not by love, as in Dante's world long before, but by obedience.

But these aspects of the work, in Taine's reproach to Milton, serve only to make the reader's labour more arduous and do not affect its essence and value. As a traveller in the next world, Milton is none the less of the same order as Dante. Unlike Dante, the medieval scholastic, he may not have known the exact location of each heavenly and earthly thing in the great Hierarchy, yet his visions are perhaps even more powerful and terrifying. Precisely because he lacked Dante's realism, Milton's are the undifferentiated, boundlessly vast landscapes of nightmare: the Underworld is a gigantic furnace whose flames offer not light but 'darkness visible'; the flight of Satan through eternity is a whirling, nebulous chaos calling to mind the pictures of Van Gogh. The serried ranks of the angels and the devils, as they line up against each other, are the most massive armies to be found in any literature.

And he managed to create a creature that has lodged itself in the imagination of the centuries: Satan. Strange as it may seem, this very religious poet expresses himself through the figure of Satan. Though he rebels against God, Satan behaves very much as the great Puritan rebel, an otherworldly Cromwell. The most moving part of the poem, aside from the Invocation of the Light, which resonates with the transfigured pain of the blind Milton, is Satan's monologue in Book I. Acknowledging the immeasurable loss he has suffered he avers that he cannot be deprived of his greatest treasure: himself:

> The mind is its own place, and in itself
> Can make a Heav'n of Hell, a Hell of Heav'n.
> What matters where if I be still the same.[2]

The monologue remains, despite all that fall, an eternal hymn to triumphant individualism, and had Milton written nothing but this, it would ensure for him a place in the pantheon of the greatest.

And the man behind it was, like his Satan, entirely worthy of his great work. As proud as the devil, the English say. Milton's essential defining feature was his exactingness, understood in some extremely noble sense. He had wished to become a priest but could not find a denomination he considered worthy of serving, and for the same reason this profoundly religious man never attended any church. Of a poet he demanded that his life, too, should have the same perfection as his verse. Taine was right when he said that few men have ensured as much respect for humanity as Milton.

His style was a mirror to his personality. His verse has a gloriously antique flavour: he banishes from the body of the poem the medieval ornament of rhyme and the Baroque bijoux of metaphor, leaving it to blank verse to drive his sentences forward. When his style is aglow with passion, it is as if Michelangelo's prophets held forth in English. It is in this work, and those of Pascal, that the century's grandeur and the exaltation and religious fervour of the Baroque can be observed at their most intense.

In *Paradise Regained*, the continuation of *Paradise Lost*, Milton is unable to sustain the level of its predecessor. He rises to such heights again only in his final work, *Samson Agonistes*, a Greek tragedy with choruses and poetry of antique dignity. In this work Milton recapitulates his themes: the unbroken defiance of the vanquished rebel; his disdain for women, those embodiments of human frailty; his admiration for the glories of antiquity; and to these he adds his lament for the passing of time:

> My race of glory run, and grace of shame
> And I shall shortly be with them that rest.[3]

Notes to Chapter 2

1. [First published in Antal Szerb, *A világirodalom története* (Budapest: Révai, 1941).]
2. [John Milton, *Paradise Lost*, Book I, ll. 254–56.]
3. [John Milton, *Samson Agonistes*, ll. 597–98.]

CHAPTER 3

The Second Romantic Generation (Byron, Shelley, Keats) (1941)[1]

Although actually only three in all these, after Shakespeare, are the greatest names in English literature: Byron, Shelley, and Keats. The sudden irruption of the three of them is a strange, miraculous episode in English literature, as irrational as Romanticism itself. They flash their way across the skies of England like a thunderbolt. Byron shapes a whole half-century after his own image, but to their contemporaries and the later average English reader Shelley and Keats remain quite incomprehensible. The Romantic sense of alienation had external reality for them too: all three felt homeless in England and spent their final years in Romantic countries: Switzerland, Italy, and Greece. They, too, like the Polish poets and Dostoevsky, were émigrés by nature.

The witty Austrian actor and cultural historian Egon Friedell called **George Gordon, Lord Byron** (1788–1824) the lead actor of the age. Byron's figure towers above the confines of literature, his works are only a part of a whole in which role and oeuvre are united. In the history of the human mind the Byron phenomenon continues to live on and exert an influence.

In comparison with life as lived by Byron our age and its writers seem like pallid houseplants or scuttling dwarfs. He bestrode life's highest peaks: he was handsome, aristocratic, rich, and possessed of a superb intellect; his every step was accompanied by outrage in his homeland and frenzied adulation worldwide; ladies fainted when he entered a room; the Pope himself took an interest in his amorous entanglements; he held court, led campaigns, and when he died Goethe mourned his passing with a funeral dirge inserted into his *Faust*. For decades he was the most important figure in Europe. And yet: he does not rank among the crowned heads of literature, or perhaps he was literature's Prince of Wales and died before he could take possession of his royal inheritance.

This life did not start off on the heights; as a child he knew the humiliations of genteel poverty and his carefully disguised lameness acquainted him early with physical pain also, and developed in him a heroic willpower that won through come what may. The family title and fortune devolved on him unexpectedly and, when that time came, the doors of Society were flung open to him, that glittering, frivolous, and hypocritical world whose poet, favourite, victim, and hopeless swain he was all his life. His youthful love affairs were the adventures, one might say, of a more spirited and demented Casanova. His short-lived marriage ended in dreadful scandal. He had to flee England. For a while he lived in Switzerland with his more spirited and congenial fellow poet and friend Shelley, and then settled in Italy. There he was overtaken by a great, all-embracing romantic love that suited his temperament for the Countess Theresa Guiccioli. It was there that the politician and hero emerged from the poet, and from here that he set out on his fatal voyage and into the Greek battle for independence.

Although all Europe awaited his every work with bated breath, beginning with the appearance of the first canto of *Childe Harold's Pilgrimage* (1812), and although the fees from this publication were enough to ensure for him the life of a lord had he not been one already, he did not consider writing his vocation; his aristocratic pride did not allow him to abandon the stance of the noble amateur and he remained a splendid dilettante. He worked quickly, carelessly, and in fits and starts; even more than Goethe he regarded writing less as work than a vital function, and not the most important one at that. His dream was to be a great statesman and a fêted icon of English society, a kind of cross between Pitt and Beau Brummell. And, as this was impossible, well — he wrote; he wrote in order to ease his mind, to vent all the bitterness of his superhuman hauteur and wounded sensibilities, so that he could dilate unimpeded on his one great theme — himself.

As a writer he was wholly self-absorbed. In every character and in every situation it was himself that he portrayed; he was the ultimate, titanic embodiment of the type of poet represented in Hungarian literature by Petőfi and Ady. This subjectivity that knew no bounds explains his influence in the age of Romanticism and also the great danger his influence represented: hundreds of thousands of little Byrons followed in his wake and strutted their unconscionable arrogance through the length and breadth of Europe.

Subjectivity does not of itself amount to sincerity; in the majority of his works Byron evinces as little sincerity as the father of Romantic subjectivity, Rousseau. As we have said, role-playing is among the indispensible features of the 'as if' poetry of Romanticism — and this histrionic feature is indeed paramount in Byron. Playing his role consistently and on a large stage, he glittered and conquered. When he sought out Bertel Thorvaldsen to make a bust of him, he assumed a grave pose full of pathos. Thorvaldsen invited him to sit more comfortably and to be as he usually was. 'But this is how I am!' exclaimed Byron, gravely offended. He identified totally with his rôle.

What exactly was this rôle? 'The man of fate' is the label we might give him. The man of fate first appears in the Gothic tales of pre-Romanticism, and becomes a living reality in the French Revolution. He has a handsome face but a gloomy expression, at once attractive and repellent. Wherever he makes an appearance, people are stunned into silence. Some grim secret broods about his person, the shadow of some grievous sin envelops him, but he endures isolation and hidden suffering with pride. In love, he brings down misfortune upon the loved one, upon souls faithful and pure, and in death, even in his final moment, he stares fate in the eye with the rebel's imperiousness.

The personal experience underlying his rôle, the dark sin for which he had to darkly suffer, was his illicit love for his half-sister, Augusta; of this was even born a child. This love it was that destroyed his marriage, was the cause of the scandal, and the reason he had to leave England. Charitable biographers have sought justifications in vain: it remains a fact — and certainly Byron would have been the first to show outrage had doubt been cast upon it. This strange and in every known respect shocking and sick emotion is part and parcel of the Byronic nature: of all Byron's loves Augusta was the most genuine passion, because only Augusta, apart from the poet himself, was truly a Byron; in loving his half-sister he loved himself and gratified his self-adoration. Without that love the Byronic pose would be cold-blooded play-acting, as was indeed the case with virtually all his acolytes, and it is through this grim love that Byron's wild excesses are validated. Byron was a poseur and even camped it up on occasion, but he never dissembled; he was a true artist.

The poems of his first period were all born of the Byronic role. That ambitious subjective travelogue, *Childe Harold's Pilgrimage* (1812–1818), transports its author's pride and sorrow all the way through the colourful regions of southern Europe: 'My greatest grief is that I leave | No thing that claims a tear'.[2] His narrative poems enjoyed as much success as *Childe Harold's Pilgrimage*: *Lara*, *The Giaour* (1813), *The Corsair*, and *The Siege of Corinth* (1816), among others. In all of these the hero is ill-starred. As for his plays, *Cain* (1816) is the fratricide drama, in which the poet is represented by the rebellious Cain and the Byronic Lucifer, while he wrote *Manfred* (1817) inspired by *Faust*. Here he comes close to uttering the name of that grave sin, sibling incest, that hounds Manfred to his proud death. Like Lara, even at the last moment Manfred rejects the consolation of religion, because within him he bears heaven and hell, the whole world, the whole of eternity, infinity:

> The mind which is immortal makes itself
> Requital for its good and evil thoughts —
> Is its own origin of ill and end
> And its own place and time.[3]

The man of fate is the progeny of Milton's Satan, in whom was first glorified pride and loneliness of individuality, and he, too, is a Satanic phenomenon. He articulates the great moral crisis of the nineteenth century: when culture gives way to civilization, that is to say, when a system of values that has endured for centuries loses its moral compass and becomes uncertain about what is good and what is evil. With the loosening of the hold of religious ideas, the Satanic reek of brimstone has by this time almost an agreeable effect on people: we are on our way to the *fin-de-siècle*, when Nietzsche proclaims the truth of the man beyond Good and Evil and Satanism becomes a necessary stimulant for decadent nerves. For the time being, however, as far as Byron is concerned, Satan still exists, heaven and hell are real, and he knows the Scriptures by heart; the Anglo-Scottish Puritan tradition lives on in him, though as it were with its polarity reversed.

When Thorvaldsen had completed his bust Byron said: 'This is not right — I am more unfortunate by far!' Byron was the foremost embodiment of the affliction of his time that we know as *Weltschmerz* (which lacks a good English translation), historically heir to pre-Romantic sentimentalism. What it lacks is that it is unmitigated by any magnanimity and sensitivity on our part. It is a more masculine, austere, and above all more defiant state of mind. *Weltschmerz* is pain on account of the world, because the world is only what it is, neither finer nor better, not adjusted to our glorious dreams. It is a simultaneously haughty and somewhat smug withdrawal into the Self's fastnesses. This is the second chapter in the history of European sorrow, the third being *fin-de-siècle* pessimism. The sentimentalist's province is the serene landscape of ruins and graveyards; that of *Weltschmerz* the sea and the wild Alps; and of pessimism urban bleakness. In cosmic terms, the sentimentalist's moment is the sunset; that of *Weltschmerz* the thunderstorm; of the pessimist autumnal rain.

But Byron amounts to far more than *Weltschmerz* and the 'man of fate'. Behind the rôle stands that other, truer Byron, of less interest to his contemporaries, but far more alive today than the rôle-player. This Byron is the late-term progeny of eighteenth-century aristocratic culture. A superior man of the world, he perhaps needs the rôle in order to play his part more effectively in society, his true stamping ground. It is with him that the figure of the 'dandy' makes its appearance in literature. The real Byron is frivolous and sarcastic, because from Castiglione's *Book of the Courtier* onwards it has not been appropriate for a man of rank to take matters over-seriously.

This other Byron found expression only gradually and with difficulty. He shows up in his satires, among which *The Vision of Judgment* stands out as a lethal offensive directed at the leading figures in contemporary English literary and political life. But actually the real Byron found his voice only in his final work, an unfinished novel in verse: *Don Juan*.

Don Juan is the story of a triumphant dandy, a Sunday's child who bestrides the peaks of life. This, too, is a poem of rebellion, more daring in fact than any of his earlier works and directed against the nineteenth century's hypocritical morality of love. It was a product of the great moral crisis of the age, intended to expose what lay behind the dignified and apparently straight-laced façade; but what an easy-flowing, elegant rebellion it is! It makes even Voltaire appear clumsy and fussy by comparison. The rebelliousness is revealed in the occasional epithet like the flash of a smile — and it is above all the structure of the stanza that breaks with the centuries-old conventions. The first six lines of the eight-line stanza are serious, good-humoured, and poetic; but the final two, a rhyming couplet, shatter the mood built up in the first six and, with a sardonic smile, unveil the reality behind the poetic image. Byron is the great artist of disillusionment, to be outshone only by his greatest disciple, Heine.

Don Juan, with its emotion and irony, its vast canvas of images and burlesque ideas, its unpredictable display of poetic beauty and amusing nonsensical rhymes, is an expression of the new *Lebensgefühl*, or feeling for life, of the fact that things are no longer as unambiguous as they once were, that there is no one truth, only truths. With his *Don Juan* Byron demolishes the fundamental edifice of classical verse: up to that point every poem expressed a particular unity of mood: it was either elevated or quotidian, cheerful or sad. Byron introduced relativity into poetry.

Even more than in *Don Juan*, the real Byron is preserved in his outstanding and enormously wide-ranging letters and diaries. In these this truly great man stands before us in all his commonplace petty-mindedness. We see how he undermines his constitution, aggravating his already exceptional irascibility by starving himself because he is worried about putting on weight; we see what a devoted friend and lover he can be but also how frankly, without any Byronic posturizing, he can give a yawn or two even in the middle of the greatest love affair; we see, stripped of all pathos, his true loneliness, and above all how genuinely and honestly his heart ached for those who suffered and were oppressed, how for him the idea of liberty was no hollow literary thesis but a fundamental reality that pervaded his whole being.

With the inevitability of fruit ripening there came into Byron's life the Greek uprising. The time had come when an attitude turns into fate, when a rôle becomes all of a sudden a life or death commitment. Those who had always championed freedom were now obliged to stand up for it. And Byron did stand up for it, though he found it somewhat diverting, too, as he found everything: he found it diverting that he, the cynical man-of-the-world, had become a heroic fighter for freedom and wrote to a woman friend: 'If I survive this campaign (and this is a "Maybe" with a capital letter in the continuation of my story) I will write two poems about it, an epic and a burlesque, and in the second I will spare no one, not even myself'. This is how he viewed things, on two levels, all his life. And yet, despite forebodings, he went off and died in a manner appropriate to a man who had always bestridden the mountain peaks, high above the crowd. The great poseur, the superficial dandy was capable of dying for the ideal that a thousand poets, far more serious and whole-hearted than he, proclaimed from behind the safety of their writing desks. His death retrospectively validates and bestows human value and dignity upon all that he wrote.

Percy Bysshe Shelley (1792–1822), Byron's friend and rival, is also a rebellious angel. His passion for freedom was more fanatical than Byron's own. He was sent down from university for writing a pamphlet entitled *The Necessity of Atheism* and later he, too, was forced by public outrage to flee England, after even his children had been removed from him when his moral character was deemed not to offer sufficient guarantee that he would bring them up as decent folk. He was to be found wherever he thought he ought to help the oppressed, he wanted to set everyone and everything free: peoples, women, love itself.

His situation was, none the less, easier than that of Byron. This curious 'angel', as his friends called him, was indeed by nature so angelic that he was a stranger to human affairs: his rebellion was as ethereal and weightless as a butterfly attacking a house. He believed mankind 'infinitely perfectible' but had not the least notion of human imperfection. In his otherworldly purity — and also in in his greatness as a poet — he is akin to Hölderlin. But Shelley was a wealthy and high-born English gentleman, and his life could not, after all, be played out in a vacuum like that of the penurious Hölderlin; he was surrounded by friends, women, children, protégés, poets — the angel was constantly dealing with people and at such times he was 'hindered in movement by his giant wings', like Baudelaire's albatross. Somehow, in everything he does, he is cack-handed; he wants to help people at all costs and in the process he upends fates, around him women commit suicide, children die, friends are alienated. A sad life, but the angel does not even notice and his poems sing forth with seraphic rapture to the very end.

He poured his pantheistic faith and moral rebellion into vast narrative and dramatic poems: *Alastor* (1815) shows how a young soul goes to the wall because it did not find in the world the high ideals it nurtured within itself — the leitmotif of Romantic *Weltschmerz*. *The Revolt of Islam* (1817), a heroic prophetic poem in twelve cantos, is an epic of universal rebellion, richly symbolic, in which it is chiefly the women who rebel. It proclaims free love; in its first draft, Laon and Cythna, the pair of lovers, are still brother and sister, for what could be more rebellious than incest between siblings? This was, however, toned down subsequently. *Prometheus Unbound* (1820) is a Greek-style drama with a chorus in the Aeschylus tradition, about cosmic rebellion in which nature itself rises up in an attempt to overthrow the rule of the age-old tyrant, Jupiter. His other drama, *The Cenci* (1819), draws on the Renaissance for its hair-raisingly transgressive theme: how Beatrice has her tyrannical father the Count Cenci murdered because he had violated her virginity.

The Cenci is a drama in the Shakespearean vein, with human characters and passions; *Julian and Maddalo* is a philosophical dialogue between Byron and Shelley; *Adonais* is a moving elegy for Keats; but the plots of his other works are difficult to follow. In these, instead of individual human beings the parts are played by crowds ('priests', 'people'), guardian spirits, allegories; serpents do battle with eagles and continents declaim poetry. Only in the most general sense could they be called narrative poems or dramas. Their action is of a supernatural, cosmic kind, resembling the movement of the stars; as we read them we see in our mind's eye the dazzling alternation of enormous beams of light and the sudden darkness of midnight over vast distances beneath jagged, measureless skies. Or we see nothing at all, and forgetting all about meaning we abandon ourselves to the sensuous music of Shelley's words.

This musicality is what is new and great about Shelley. It is Shelley who brings the vivid and restless cavalcade of colour and rhyme into the modern poem. As Mihály Babits says: 'Shelley soars as high as it is possible for human language to soar. His poetry is sheer ethereality. Words are relieved of their weight and material dross. The variety of his metres and their melodic complexity is inexhaustible, a richness the like of which has not existed since the time of the Greeks'.

Of his shorter poems, the *Ode to the West Wind* is outstanding. No paraphrase could convey the brilliance of its music and mood. In this poem all of nature becomes verbal music, the entire greatness of autumn sings out in all its voices; no poet before or since has been so much an instrument played by the hands of the Universe:

> Make me thy lyre, even as the forest is:
> What if my leaves are falling like its own!
> The tumult of thy mighty harmonies
> Will take from both a deep, autumnal tone,
> Sweet though in sadness.[4]

The poet asks the west wind to disperse his soul into the far corners of the universe, so that his word may reach everyone everywhere and proclaim that after winter spring will surely come.

Like Byron and Keats, Shelley died young. His light boat tumbled into the stormy Gulf of Spezia, his body was cast ashore with Keats's book of poems in his pocket — that is how his body was identified. Byron had his corpse cremated on the shore, though his heart was not burned but laid to eternal rest under the pyramid of Cestius in Rome, with the noble inscription, *Cor cordium*.[5]

It was here that **John Keats** (1795–1821) had lain at rest since the previous year. The third great English Romantic was not of such fortunate birth as the others. Keats was impecunious, sickly, and ugly, and never enjoyed success. Apart from the Elgin marbles recently brought to England, he knew of Greek beauty only from pen sketches in an encyclopedia; he never received much higher education; and he knew no Greek. His first poems were assassinated by the critics as meaningless gibberish. His only love, a coquettish and empty-headed slip of a girl, failed to stand by the distressed, penniless poet and caused him only pain. While caring for his consumptive brother he became consumptive himself, went to Rome to recuperate, and there in Rome starved to death. His greatness as a poet was recognized only half a century later, by the Pre-Raphaelites who celebrated in him one of their forebears.

But in the short time given to him, he loved life intensely. Among the Romantics, who fled from life with their heads in the clouds, he was the exception, who with his eyes, heart, and every fibre of his being was open to beauty of every kind. He loved life not with the sweeping Rabelaisian gesture, nor with the sickly longing of the decadents, but in the way that a flower loves the sun. In his poems he never tires of recording how many beautiful things there are in the world:

> Such the sun, the moon,
> Trees old and young, sprouting a shady boon
> For simple sheep; and such are daffodils
> With the green world they live in; and clear rills
> That for themselves a cooling covert make
> 'Gainst the hot season; the mid forest brake,
> Rich with a sprinkling of fair musk-rose blooms:
> And such too is the grandeur of the dooms
> We have imagined for the mighty dead.[6]

The beauties of literature aroused in him breathtaking ecstasy; he wrote magnificent sonnets about his fellow poets and his own feelings on reading Homer and *King Lear*. He was, in his way, very happy. In his letters he kept searching for the ideal of happiness, attempting to establish gradations of joy; or he writes: 'I had an idea that a Man might pass a very pleasant life in this manner — Let him on a certain day read a certain page of full Poesy or distilled Prose, and let him wander upon it, and bring home to it, and prophesy upon it, and dream upon it... Now it appears to me that almost any Man may like the spider spin from his own inwards his own airy Citadel'.[7] He wrote that he loved beautiful sentences in the manner of a lover.

Beauty is all. Keats is the first and the greatest in the long line of English poet-aesthetes. By beauty he means something more profound and more comprehensive than the others. Though he is the least abstract of the great Romantics, his philosophy is the most profound. Because he too is, in his own way, a philosophical poet and seeks the place of beauty in metaphysics: ' "Beauty is truth, truth beauty" ', — 'that is all | Ye know on earth, and all ye need to know'.

Only beauty can open up for us the way to knowledge of the only truth worth knowing; not the truth that can be grasped in moral lessons in the manner of Wordsworth, or indeed be formulated in words at all, but that opens up only to the inner eye, reconciling us to fate and imbuing us with oppressive zeal or the mature joy of autumn.

And this beauty is eternal: 'A thing of Beauty is a joy for ever.' This is the lesson of his long narrative poem *Endymion*, and of one of the world's most beautiful poems, the *Ode on a Grecian Urn*. The image on the Grecian urn preserves for all time a moment of life's beauty:

> Ah, happy, happy boughs! that cannot shed
> Your leaves, nor ever bid the Spring adieu;
> And, happy melodist, unwearied,
> For ever piping songs for ever new.[8]

On the urn the desire of the youth chasing his beloved remains eternally beautiful and eternally longing, unlike the passion of the living 'that leaves a heart high — sorrowful, [...] a burning forehead, and a parching tongue'. Life goes on, but *the form is eternal* — it is our only bulwark against the march of time, our only immortality.

Keatsian beauty embraces not only delicate and superficial beauty; in this he differs from the aesthetes that were to follow. Suffering, too, is beauty.

'The excellence of every Art,' he writes, 'is its intensity, capable of making all disagreeable evaporate, from being in close relationship with Beauty and Truth — Examine King Lear & you will find this *exemplified* throughout.'[9]

In his fine book *Keats and Shakespeare* John Middleton Murry analyses what Keats means by intensity: a state of the most profound understanding, the moment when the hidden meaning of the world is revealed to the poet and visionary. This is the meaning of these tragic lines of Keats: 'Verse, Fame, and Beauty are intense indeed, | But Death intenser, — Death is Life's high meed'.

Death is the most intense moment and the most poetic, and to reach Keats's creative heights requires the permanent proximity to death that Keats endured.

In that intensity everything abstract and diffuse, everything that can be expressed in other ways, is purged from the poem like dross, and all that remains is pure poetry, the expression of the soul and the vision itself. Such are Keats's magnificent odes, sonnets, and ballads: *Ode to a Nightingale, To Autumn, Ode on Melancholy, On Sitting Down to Read King Lear Once Again, To Ailsa Rock, In Drear-Nighted December, La Belle Dame Sans Merci*, and his last sonnet, *Bright star...*, among others.

The more straightforward of his longer narrative poems (*Lamia, The Eve of St Agnes, Isabella*) owe their power to the restless Baroque splendour of their language, but of greater merit are his reflective poems, *Endymion* and especially *Hyperion*. It is very difficult to explain what either of these is about, their narrative being no less vague than Shelley's. Had *Hyperion* been completed, it would have been his life's finest achievement. The poet, now in poor health, tried twice to complete it but failed. In reading the second version we feel as with the later work of Hölderlin: in his 'intensity' the poet is speaking of truths that are beyond the limits of our perception, and we are seized by the *horror sacri*. It is a curious coincidence that both visionaries, independently of each other, chose the name Hyperion.

Shelley scaled the highest peaks in terms of the poem's musicality, Keats in terms of its picturesqueness. It is astonishing how much is compressed into each line of Keats, how many images, how many associations of disparate ideas, how much hidden meaning. His poems can be savoured virtually word by word. Perhaps this is the secret of his magic: a single word is 'a thing of Beauty', a beautiful objet d'art in its rightful place. For those who know English these three celebrated lines are 'a joy for ever':

> The same that oft-times hath
> Charm'd magic casements, opening on the foam
> Of perilous seas, in faery lands forlorn.[10]

No translation can convey how much of a fairy-tale Middle Ages, how much dream and legend, are encompassed in the words *casement, faery, perilous,* and how the entire stanza is borne in wave-like motion towards dreamy infinity by the final, postposed epithet: *forlorn.*

Or how are we to analyse the perfection of his epithets: autumn as the season of mists and 'mellow' fruitfulness, the 'rich' anger of his beloved, the reader of King Lear must 'burn through [...] betwixt damnation and impassion'd clay'. In terms of versification, too, he is innovatory in the density of his recourse to enjambement, with the phrase or sentence running on through successive lines and not terminating on the rhyme or line end (this Romantic innovation was later adopted in French verse by Victor Hugo), and also in his opening up of the closed sonnet by means of a concluding image, but one that pointed away into the far distance. But to paraphrase the miracle of his poems, to approach them theoretically, is as hopeless as in the case of great musical works. Poems should be read, not explicated.

Byron, Keats, and Shelley all died tragically young. They did not achieve maturity, they did not — after an impassioned and rebellious youth — become sober-minded classics, like the distinguished poets of Germany. This kind of calm composure is, alas, always something of a betrayal — a betrayal with respect to youth, with respect to the unutterable message that the poet can, while still young, incorporate directly into his poetry. By dying young these three great English poets kept their faith with rebellion: they did not make peace and they did not compromise. Their figures are wreathed in the nimbus of eternal youth, like those 'coming to the sacrifice' on the Grecian urn in Keats's greatest ode.

Notes to Chapter 3

1. [First published in Antal Szerb, *A világirodalom története* (Budapest: Révai, 1941).]
2. [George Gordon, Lord Byron, *Childe Harold's Pilgrimage*, Book I, ll. 180–81.]
3. [Byron, *Manfred*, Act III, Scene 4, ll. 150–53.]
4. [Percy Bysshe Shelley, *Ode to the West Wind*, ll. 55–59].
5. [The fate of Shelley's dead body was, in fact, more complicated. It seems his heart was kept by Mary Shelley until the end of her days.]
6. [John Keats, *Endymion* I, ll. 14–22.]
7. [Keats, letter to John Hamilton Reynolds, 19 February 1818.]
8. [Keats, *Ode on a Grecian Urn*, ll. 21–24.]
9. [Keats, letter to George and Tom Keats, 22 December 1817].
10. [Keats, *Ode to a Nightingale*, ll. 68–70.]

CHAPTER 4

Rousseau (1929)[1]

The Return to Nature and, through Sensibility, to Ourselves

In the vast *oeuvre* of Jean-Jacques Rousseau (1712–1778) there is little that holds interest for the present-day reader, but the first volume of his *Confessions* remains to this day one of his most fascinating and pleasurable works. It brings to life the Switzerland and the south of France as they once were, the picturesque landscapes where the young Jean-Jacques, as indulged child and carefree vagabond, lived a blissful life, implementing his dreams of freedom, love, and simplicity. It is easy enough for the reader to appreciate why Rousseau continued for the rest of his life to yearn for this Eden of his youth and that his later life assumed the form of retrospection and the desire to 'return'.[2]

In 1750 Rousseau published his famous work, in which he pronounced the magic word and became the Romantic movement's liberator and saviour. This magic word was: 'return'. All humanity's ills began when it turned away from Nature, and the only remedy was to return to it.[3]

Nature, the great Inspirer, that formidable idol before whom the cream of the Romantic century burned incense, the great evangelizer who has been strewing her false promises perhaps ever since humanity was charred by civilization's shirt of Nessus. To return to Nature: the Alexandrian age, the bucolic atmosphere of Theocrates, the Arcadia of the Renaissance, all of these are so many literary manifestations of that yearning. In the life of the individual, too, that same yearning often makes an appearance, accompanied by a degree of unsocial sentiment, at times when we feel our situation vis-à-vis our fellows has become, as a result of the network of dependencies and mirrored copycat behaviour, so hopelessly complicated that it seems best to sever all relations and run off and take refuge in some Rousseauesque primeval forest.

This state of asocial irascibility, which the profoundly neurotic Rousseau experienced with the intensity of a persecution complex, is the most straightforward psychological explanation for 'the return':

> Discontented with your present state, for reasons which threaten your unfortunate descendants with still greater discontent, you will perhaps wish it were in your power *to go back*; and this feeling should be a panegyric on your first ancestors, a criticism of your contemporaries, and a terror to the unfortunates who will come after you.[4]

In the Rousseauesque 'return' the negative aspect of our flight from society is counterbalanced by a positive tendency, a striving to go in a specific direction, leading to our perception of our longings in Nature, a process known in psychology as projection. Nature is tranquil because our life in Court and City is an everlasting struggle; Nature is benign because our fellows are evil; Nature is beautiful, like our eternal beloved, whom we seek in vain.

Rousseau made us aware of this projection, which he, too, had experienced: he pointed out that when we flee from the world we find in Nature the very longings we have ourselves projected: in effect, it is ourselves we find. 'But what did I enjoy when I was alone? *Myself, the whole universe* [...] I gathered around me everything that could flatter my heart; my desires were the measure of my pleasures'.[5]

'*Myself, the whole universe*': the two are one. The unity of Self and Nature, the fundamental tenet of the later, increasingly sophisticated natural philosophy of the Germans is, for Rousseau, the most straightforward thing in the world; it is a given. Nature had dwelt in hearts previously to this, but only as a luxury of the spirit, a mood accompanying hours of solitude, or the inspiration of picaresque adventures; now, thanks to such evidence, love of nature is raised to the level of a fundamental moral principle. If Self and Nature are one, we must always listen to what our Self has to say, because it is the word of Nature. There is another psychological factor to be taken into consideration here. Every thinking human being knows the anguish of the mental chaos when every thought leads to inconsistencies, when an excess of cogitation causes a divorce from reality and there seems no possible way to proceed. At such times there comes to the fore an outrageous longing to jettison everything hitherto thought and return to the most basic elements — the facts. It could be said that factual evidence is thought of a kind I no longer think, but feel. In a century when people were impatient with thought and every system of logic had been corroded by Voltaire-style scepticism and Montesquieu-style relativism, Rousseau urged a return of the intellect: a return to feeling, to factual evidence. 'Once one is prepared to listen to one's inner voice, everyone can feel what is good, everyone can discern what is beautiful; there is no need for anyone to teach us either the one or the other'.[6]

Through Rousseau therefore it is not only the Nature cult of that age but also respect for feeling that acquire a new and identical meaning, which is the return to the Self. Finding the universe and Truth within our own selves is the chief tenet of all mysticism: 'Noli foras ire, redi in te ipsum,' says St Augustine.[7] Nonetheless, the Rousseauesque return and Christian introspection are poles apart, at opposite ends of the moral cosmos. Puritanism subsists between heaven and hell, stepping each day onto a crossroads; when Pietism turns inwards, the inner voice is not only the word of forgiveness but also the inimical temptations of the flesh. Christian mysticism is dualistic: the medieval saints are challenged alternately by the truthful angels and envoys of the Father of Lies; the new age carries within it two conflicting worlds or, in the words of St Paul, two sets of laws.

Rousseau's self carries within it only one world: the appeal that comes from his inner Self, whatever is dictated by feelings, all derive from Nature and are all good. Seillière rightly points out that Rousseau laicized quietism: the quietists taught that the soul must surrender in total passivity to the instructions of God or, according to Rousseau, to those of feelings, of our inner Self.[8] The path of Christian mysticism, for all its unpredictability and forgiving nature, is still an active path of sorts with, as its abiding symbols, the pilgrims Dante and Bunyan. Rousseau's mysticism, fully attuned to the temper of his age, is entirely passive; his return is no pilgrim's way but rather an unobtrusive descent down some incline, towards the dark abyss.

Passive self-surrender is inseparable from the Rousseauesque return and part and parcel of all things pre-Romantic. Rousseau proclaims the rights of the passions and, lo and behold, after so many centuries of struggle and heroism, the soul seems overwhelmed by what, according to La Rochefoucauld, is our chief passion: sloth. To be natural means actually to be slothful. This is the sense in which Rousseau imagines the ideal primeval humans to be natural: they are inactive, without ambition, passive. Lasserre hits the nail on the head when he says: 'Had humankind ever been as originally depicted by Rousseau, he would have remained forever foolish'.[9]

The Return through Ourselves to the Child, the Mother, and Annihilation

If we follow the Rousseauesque return, self-surrender will lead us farther. The return to the Self — but our Self is built of so many conflicting layers. To which of those, then, are we to return? Self-surrender has a gravitational pull that will naturally tend to drive it towards the lowest and deepest of them.

It is not to the individual personality that the Rousseauesque return urges us. This, our personality, results from a combination of historical forces and pedagogical influences as well as a continuous and ever more perfect adjustment to the outside world. Its role is to preserve and fully validate itself vis-à-vis that outside world through continual energetic interaction. It is not to this active, social self that Rousseau wishes to return: indeed, that is exactly what he is fleeing.

Perhaps, then, it is to our intellectual essence, which already reigns in spiritual freedom over a world whose clamour has become, by the time it reaches the heights, no more than refined, abstract harmonies? No: thought is cold, fallible, not natural: over thought feeling enjoys supremacy.

The Rousseauesque return is a flight from the outside world, from our own reactions to it, to the cellars, at which the continuous aerial bombardment that is the world fires its slings and arrows after us in vain.

The soul's innate slothfulness serves, in fact, a very important, one might even say biological, purpose and in times of crisis often saves the soul's life. At those times when the world is infinitely bleak and offers nothing to long for and thus stimulate us to go on living (for not to long is not to be alive), slothfulness suggests a solution: the soul, obeying its own gravitational pull, relapses into its earlier yearnings and is sustained by them. This is *regression*. The most powerful variety of regression is the rekindling of our childhood condition.

'Discontented with your present state... you will perhaps wish it were in your power to go back!' says Rousseau. He would like to regress to the ancestors, to the caveman, to something totally primeval, to his primitive self, to a period he had actually lived through, to the starting point: to his childhood.

Rousseau is synonymous with the cult of the child. It is well known that Rousseau 'discovered' maternal love for the upper classes and for literature. Before he appeared on the scene an aristocratic Frenchwoman saw her children only at the morning *lever*, when they were shepherded in to kiss her hand and then hurried out again. The situation of children in the eighteenth century was appalling: the scions of princes and princesses would flee the parental home because what they were fed on was wafer-thin and could put up with going hungry no longer.[10]

Rousseau made children fashionable. He is one of those responsible for the widely held misapprehension that childhood is a happy time. According to the Greeks, including Aristotle, children are not happy, happiness being available only to those who have achieved their fullness, their entelechy. Indeed, they did not set great store by childhood: in their eyes a child is not yet, but only potentially, a person.

However, Rousseau turned this commonsense judgement on its head: in his view it is precisely the child who had achieved fullness of being — the adult has merely regressed. Children listen to their natural instincts, while adults are enslaved to convention; adults are evil, whereas children, being natural, are good, innocent, and an example to us.

Clearly, as with his view of Nature, projection is at work here, too: Rousseau projected back into childhood his ideal of the free, natural, and tranquil life. But in this case the projection has more substance, because there is some truth in it. Children are indeed natural in that they are dedicated to their instincts. They have no regard for their fellows and their passions are not inhibited by unhealthy ideas: the child is a creature of passion. That, according to Rousseau is why the child is happy — and, according to modern psychology, unhappy. His life is an unending confrontation with inflexible rules, all the more cruel because he cannot yet understand them.

But Rousseau had observed not actual children, only himself, his own inner child. He could feel welling up again in him the longings of childhood and proclaimed the child happy because the child is closer, after all, to implementing those longings. Because his yearnings were a child's, he felt himself to be immensely pure and good: he wrote several times that he was the best human being that had ever walked this earth.

Rousseau said this in good faith, convinced that children's yearnings are pure and good because he had never observed real children at close quarters. The ruthless self-analysis, shorn of all emotion and self-pity, that is the only path to self-knowledge was alien to his mild disposition. He was ignorant of what a later pre-Romantic poet, William Blake, would see all too clearly:

> The Infant Joy is beautiful, but its anatomy
> Horrible, ghast & deadly! nought shalt thou find in it,
> But dark despair & everlasting brooding melancholy![11]

We cannot shirk from dissecting the content of that childhood yearning to which Rousseau regressed. Our analysis will lead us down into those dark and terrifying mines where only the Davy lamp of psychology casts some uncertain light. We approach with trepidation what seems to us the truth and should like to draw attention to a single instance in which we believe the key to Rousseau's entirely characteristic nature is to be found.

We have in mind a passage from a well-known section of the *Confessions*: Mme de Warens is at last ready to take Rousseau into her good graces unreservedly. The young Rousseau, however, suddenly sees in Mme de Warens his own mother and dissolves into tears.[12] Thus that child's yearning on account of which Jean-Jacques wished to regress into childhood, and to him subconsciously synonymous with childhood, was the longing for a mother. The fact that he had lost his mother at a very early age is immaterial: it is our very first impressions in life that are imprinted most strongly upon us. Perhaps it is because when he should have been and could not be a 'mother's boy' that Jean-Jacques longed for this all his life. By Mme de Warens's side he found what he had been longing for, and after he had to leave her spent the rest of his life searching for tenderness, a protective wing, to have his whole being swathed in the soft, womanly cotton-wool stuffing of womanliness. He would have liked the whole world to treat him in a motherly way and when that refused to happen, he fell out with that wicked world and took refuge in his fantasies of childhood. In his childhood, a time when though the world was likewise unmotherly but he was not yet much bothered by reality, as his all-powerful child's imagination made up for everything.

And yet: we have still not reached the ultimate stage of regression. The longing underlying the yearning for a mother is a longing for the *pre-individual state of being*. A child not yet separated from his mother and whose every activity is determined by her is not yet an individual. The dreadful awareness of responsibility borne by the individual life does not yet weigh on his shoulders: just as a branch is still of a piece with the tree, so, through his mother, is the child of a piece with his species, his family. His actions have not yet repercussions on himself, his soul is not yet engulfed by the world in the guise of fears, he is protectively clasped in the arms of parental omnipotence.

Pre-individual existence is actually not yet human life, which is a solitary struggle against external forces, a daily renewed single combat for the narrow slot in time and space the individual has been allotted. Pre-individual existence means to renounce the solitariness that makes a being human, so that he relapses into an animal oneness with mother and species to renounce the struggle, in time and space, again to sink into the unfathomable chaos, the primeval sea upon which, in the view of Schopenhauer, humankind rows in the boat of the *principium individuationis*. It is the *néant*, the *mēon* ('non-being'), annihilation, death. To return to pre-individual existence is to return to the 'melancholy night of nothingness' from which we emerge at birth.

In between the darkness in which it begins and ends comes a brief moment of heroic struggle, which is human life, and it is the longing for life that endows the human being with the strength to continue this ultimately hopeless battle. In anyone whose longing for life grows faint another longing necessarily takes a hold: that for the darkness of the beginning, which is at the same time the darkness of the end. The death wish: this is the final stage of Rousseauesque regression.

Lasserre, with amazing perceptiveness, articulated the relationship between the mother concept and the death wish: 'Rousseau's insult to the most glorious achievements of humanity leads step by step to the creative principles of nature, right to those eternal "Mothers" who, Goethe imagined, stand guard in the depths of the unknown over every form of being'.[13] The Mothers in *Faust Part II* are Goethe's most obscure symbols, dimly suggestive of the primeval secrets of existence in the dawning twilight of his genius. It is to them, who safeguard and have possession of the lives of things unborn, that Rousseauesque strivings wing back and against them that Rousseauesque subterranean attacks are directed. To use the language of the child's imagination: he blames his mother for bringing him into the world and the forces of Nature for expelling him from the Paradise of non-existence to which there is no return save death.

Mitten in dem Leben sind wir vom Tode umfangen, in the midst of life we are in the embrace of death. Death does not approach us only from without and head-on, along our lives' path, with the quiet certainty of the hourglass, but from within and behind, too, erected by our secret desires. We have a tendency to consider the poets' death wish disingenuous, yet underlying our most commonplace longings lurks a greater longing but one to which the life instinct does not allow the dignity of naming itself. We are not conscious that it is when, exhausted by our labours, we long for a prolonged rest, to lay ourselves down and lie for days on end doing and thinking nothing, talking to no one, that a longing for the ultimate repose gathers emotional impetus. We desire death when in a crowd, a procession, a political rally, because in the mass exhilaration we desire to relinquish our individuality, as in death; it is death that we seek in every exhilaration that offers ecstasy and divests us of our ego: it is death that we seek above all in the exhilaration of love, which the poets have since time immemorial expressed by the symbol of death. We speak of being in love in deadly earnest, believe we are going to die because of unrequited love, although love requited constitutes a greater danger. And when we determinedly and with incongruous joy abandon ourselves to the passions that cut short our days, the death wish triumphs over the life instinct. When we abandon ourselves to the sweet sorrows that inspire poetry and music, we hear always death's siren song:

> In every truly solemn hour
> That made thine earthly form to quiver,
> I touched thy soul's foundation ever [...][14]

says Death in Hofmannstahl's drama, *The Fool and Death* (*Die Tor und der Tod*).

It is difficult to create awareness of this longing, as Christian culture has been trying for 2000 years to eradicate it from our consciousness. Christianity has sublimated the death wish: above the human being desirous of escaping from earthly life it has spread heaven, the everlasting life of the hereafter. Our despairing human pursuit of self-annihilation has been transformed into a holy hankering for the hereafter. As a result of the enormously forceful discipline of our culture we even now feel the death wish to be somehow unseemly.

In human beings two opposing forces wage a continually renewed battle: one is the urge to go on living, the other the lure of the tranquillity of nonexistence with its siren song that wafts to magical effect from the still waters of childhood. It cannot be claimed that the life-urge is natural and the other not: indeed, in physical terms, the instinct towards annihilation is the more natural. It is the message of the body, of that body of ours which daily inches closer to annihilation. 'The impulse of our elements is towards deoxidation. Life is compelled oxidation,' writes Novalis, the greatest poet of decay. Life is a continuous effort to stay alive, the willpower to overcome the physical laws of nature; and within heroic humanity's own self resides that greatest enemy, that other desire, that hydra whose self-renewing head needs to be struck off every day.

Rousseau's great act of liberation consisted in his probing deeply the various pre-Romantic tendencies, and his setting free, making mentionable, and bringing to the surface of the mind the yearning for and the symbols of annihilation: malignant Nature, deadly passion, the longings — concealed, but all the more urgent for that — of his century, the sweetness of thousand-faceted nirvana. In his wake the European spirit trod the path to regression and the poetry of the second half of the eighteenth century is one mighty symphony of death, the like of which the world had not experienced since the time of the *danse macabre* and the flagellants. It is to such an inauspicious, grim, and yet enigmatically attractive tune that the European spirit launched that great about-turn that we call Romanticism.

Death and Rebirth

> Man looks with emotion down into the far, low-lying time, when the spindle of his life ran round as yet almost naked without threads; for his beginning borders more nearly upon his end than the middle, and the outward bound and homeward bound coasts of our life hang over into the dark sea. — JEAN PAUL.[15]

Present-day French criticism is deeply antipathetic to Rousseau: "ce malheureux" is the mildest of the epithets applied to him. Rousseau undermined the foundations of classicism, of French culture par excellence. In terms of theory Rousseau paved the way for the French Revolution and the Rousseauesque mood, the passive surrender of the self to the longing for annihilation so diminished the energies of the French aristocracy that they had nothing to offer the Revolution apart from passive heroism: to go to the guillotine with heads held high. French pre-Romanticism was the grandiose suicide of the upper classes; while French Romanticism, which bourgeoned after the Revolution, was according to the new critics no longer French, being neither aristocratic nor classical, but rather the barbaric infiltration of the Germanic spirit that Rousseau's cosmopolitanism had allowed into the Le Nôtre garden of French culture.

What kills one cures another. While for French culture pre-Romanticism spelled destruction, for other nations it was a rebirth.

Thus, by means first and foremost of the doctrine that a person who is 'natural' — uneducated and in tune with his instincts — is of more value than one hidebound by convention, self-confidence was restored to those nations that had until then groaned under the oppressive knowledge that French culture is superior, like younger siblings intimidated by their elder brother's superior wisdom. 'The less civilized parts of Europe could not miss the opportunity,' writes Charles Maurras, 'to recognize and love themselves in the child of Nature, out of which Paris had carved itself a worshipped idol'.[16]

Smaller nations in particular found the Rousseauesque idea a boon. In fact, only now did they find their rightful places in the concerted European spirit. So long as French culture was considered the sole, objective, and ultimate goal, an unconditional paradigm, all that the small nations could strive to produce was a pale imitation of French culture. Pre-Romanticism liberated the small nations and handed them back their national cultures.

It is true that, before Rousseau, Switzerland had already launched the pre-Romantic movement, with Salomon Gessner and Albrecht von Haller in poetry and Johann Jakob Bodmer and Johann Jakob Breitinger in criticism. Nonetheless it was Rousseau's Swiss origins that placed that small country in the limelight and it was enthusiasm for him that created the Swiss tourism that laid the material foundations which allowed this small peasant republic to develop into a first-class centre of culture.[17] Poland received its constitution from Rousseau; Scandinavia and Scotland were discovered for Europe by the pre-Romantic temper. But the great Germanic nations, too, were liberated from French tutelage at this time and restored to their national cultures.[18]

In what follows we shall be examining the rebirth of national cultures that derived from the Rousseauesque idea so as ultimately to comprehend the rebirth of Hungary. A return of self-confidence is scarcely an adequate explanation on its own, although the more advantageous position that Rousseau outlined for nations in the intellectual cosmos certainly had a decisive influence. As in the life of an individual, so in that of a nation, too, self-confidence is needed to provide the strength and courage to think a thought through to its conclusion. Without self-confidence, or, more grandly, self-belief, a thought when encountering other, conflicting thoughts, comes to a frightened, halfway standstill and suffers the fate of all half-thought-out thoughts: it goes tumbling down into the subconscious where it becomes distorted into an anguished *idée fixe* in the way gods who are no longer believed in turn into phantoms.

Self-assurance, however, is merely a blind intellectual force, not in itself intellectual substance. It is of primary importance to think ideas through. Having followed pre-Romantic thought in its decline to the depths plumbed by Rousseau, we must now press on, as with Rousseau we are not yet at our terminus. We need to follow the spirit on the trajectory of its inner logic, which of course does not mean that the ideas to be developed here are ones that were systematically thought through by Rousseau, Herder or anyone else in the Romantic period: maybe they were, maybe not, but that is unimportant. Here the issue is not the thoughts of individuals but the spirit in the process of its fulfilment, the thought in its own thinking process as it occasionally makes a partial appearance in the awareness of certain thinkers. What we are after is the history not of thinkers but of thought, which achieves complete reality not in individuals but in ages and nations viewed globally: in Europe.

Rousseau's destructiveness, his nihilism, his sin lay in his failure to think his idea through to the end, and this is why he became not a divine but a demonic force in the history of the French spirit. He had touched rock bottom and lacked the forcefulness to work his way back up on the crest of spiritual causality. The spirit achieves reality in polar opposites, each concept bringing its antithesis in its wake: nadir-zenith, death-life. Rousseau attained only one extreme.

How closely the longings for annihilation and rebirth are intertwined in the soul is easy to document in terms of both psychology and philology. The psychological evidence comes in the form of depression and premeditated suicide. In desperation human beings turn in upon themselves, break with an outside world that has lost all meaning for them. In the case of healthy minds, after a while despair reaches its nadir and there is then a sudden turn-around: out of the blue, without any outside intervention, the spirit finds consolation; it re-evaluates the world, notices that what had previously made it despair is not, after all, a fatal blow, and that the world from which it had recently turned away as alien still offers much in the way of consolation and meaning. At the fatal hour, some mysterious wellspring opens up, from which fresh new vigour gushes forth.

On the philological side, countless examples from the world of religious history and mythology attest to the symbolic expression of the unity of death and resurrection; hence, first and foremost, Christian eschatology. But every people has its own stories of journeys in the under- and afterworld to tell. At the time of the great plague the Chinese emperor-god's son descends into the underworld and, wearing a gold mask, brings up with him the laws of the new empire. The Egyptian Book of the Dead relates the wanderings of the deceased through the deserts of annihilation, where he has many trials to undergo before he reaches the greatest of all, when before the judgement seat of Osiris and the deity of Mysteries and Miracles, Hermes Trismegistus, the measure of his heart is taken: if he is found pure he may board Osiris's boat, bound for eternity. The Greek Orpheus descends into the underworld to bring Eurydice back to life, and Demeter to bring back Persephone: their underworld journeys lie at the heart of the later Greek mystery plays. One last example: before he reaches Paradise Dante's journey, too, leads through the Inferno.

Pre-Romanticism, too, with Rousseau as company, ranged the underworld, the realms of annihilation, and the world of the subconscious, where there is no longer any individuality to be found: many did not prove equal to the test and were found impure when weighed in the balance of Hermes Trismegistus.

Notes to Chapter 4

1. [First published in Antal Szerb, *Magyar preromantika* [Hungarian Pre-romanticism] (Budapest: Dunántúli Nyomda, 1929).]
2. Cf. Emile Faguet, *Dix-huitième siècle. Études littéraires*, Paris, 1890.
3. Cf. 'Rückkehr gerade der Grundgedenke der Romantik war.' Fritz Strich, *Deutsche Klassik und Romantik oder Vollendung und Unendlichkeit. Ein Vergleich*, München, 1922; p. 310.
4. [Jean-Jaqcues Rousseau, *Discourse on the Origin of Inequality*, Part I, trans. by G. D. H. Cole (New York: Cosimo Classics, 2005), p. 25 ('Mécontent de ton état présent, par des raisons qui annoncent à la Postérité malheureuse de plus grands mécontentements encore, peut-être voudrois-tu pouvoir *rétrograder*; Et ce sentiment doit faire l'Éloge de tes premiers aïeux, la

critique de tes contemporains, et l'effroi de ceux, qui auront le malheur de vivre après toi',
Szerb's emphasis).]

5. [Jean-Jacques Rousseau, *Third Letter to M. de Malesherbes*, 26 January 1752, trans. by
Peter Abbs, <https://philosophynow.org/issues/68/The_Full_Revelation_of_the_Self_Jean-
Jacques_Rousseau_and_the_Birth_of_Deep_Autobiography> [accessed 17 July 2016] ('Mais de
quoi jouissais-je enfin quand j'étais seul? *De moi, de l'univers entier* [...] Je rassemblais autour de
moi tout ce qui pouvait flatter mon coeur, mes désirs étaient la mesure de mes plaisirs', Szerb's
emphasis).]

6. [Translation by Peter Sherwood ('Sitôt qu'on veut rentrer en soi-même, chacun sent ce qui est
bien, chacun discerne ce qui est beau; nous n'avons pas besoin qu'on nous apprenne à connaître
ni l'un ni l'autre', Jean-Jacques Rousseau, *La Nouvelle Héloïse,* Letter 13 to Julie).]

7. [Do not wish to go outside, turn back into yourself.]

8. Ernest Seillière, *Jean-Jacques Rousseau*, Paris, 1921.

9. Pierre Lasserre, *Le Romantisme français*, Paris, 1907; p. 58.

10. Hippolyte Taine, *Les Origines de la France contemporaine*, Paris, 1876. Vol. I.

11. [William Blake, *Jerusalem*, Plate 22, 22–24, in Erdman, p. 167.]

12. Jean-Jacques Rousseau, *Confessions*. In *Oeuvres complètes*, [Paris: Armand-Aubrée], 1829, pp.
249–50. ['Je ne sais quelle invincible tristesse en empoissonait le charme. J'étois comme si j'avois
commis un inceste. Deux ou trois fois, en la pressant avec transport dans mes bras, j'inondai son
sein de mes larmes', Jean-Jacques Rousseau, *Confessions*, I, Ch. 5.]

13. Lasserre, p. 33.

14. [Hugo von Hofmannstahl, *The Fool and Death*, trans. by Elisabeth Walter ('In jeder wahrhaft
grossen Stunde | Die schauern deine Erdenform gemacht, | Hab ich dich angerührt im
Seelengrunde'.]

15. Jean Paul, *Titan II.* 115. *Titan: A Romance*, trans. by Charles T. Brooks, 1864; p. 315–16 ['Der
Mensch sieht-bewegt in die tiefe Zeit hinunter, so seine Lebensspindel fast noch nackt ohne
Faden umlief; denn sein Anfang grenzt näher als die Mitte an sein Ende und die aus- und
einschiffende Küste unseres Leben hängt ins dunkle Meer'].

16. Charles Maurras, *Romantisme et révolution* [Paris: Nouvelle Librairie Nationale, 1928], p. 6
[*recte* 7].

17. Between 1760 and the French Revolution alone, Switzerland was the topic of more than 80
works published in 130 editions that appeared in France. Daniel Mornet, *Le Romantisme en France
au XVIIIe siècle*, Paris, 1912; p. 63.

18. Maurras, p. 49.

CHAPTER 5

Don Juan's Secret (1940)[1]

The name of Don Juan, so familiar to us all, first crops up in the seventeenth century. As 'Don Juan de Tenorio' he appears in a play ascribed to Tirso de Molina entitled *El burlador de Sevilla y convidado de piedra*, and for centuries Don Juan is the name by which he has been known, on stage and in our minds.[2]

Reading the old Spanish play recently I made a surprising discovery, something that I have not seen mentioned in any study of the Don Juan legend. I was quite astonished to realize that Don Juan does not seduce any of his victims, in the sense that we understand the word today. That is to say: he does not beguile any of them with his manly charms in order to make the unfortunate maiden lose her head and stray from the path of virtue, like *Faust*'s Gretchen and her innumerable literary progeny. When the play opens it is pitch dark and Don Juan is taking his leave of a lady who only now realizes that in the dark she has been entertaining someone other than the person she had expected and is mortified that her guest has been Don Juan. Thus, Don Juan has made his conquest not with his masculine good looks but with the complicity of the dark. He repeats this ploy once more in the course of the play. He also has his way with a naive peasant girl by promising marriage; and he conquers another by using his aristocratic demeanour to intimidate her groom on their wedding day: the young man gives up his bride so that she can marry the Don. To Donna Anna, too, he promises marriage. So it is not that the women in the play cannot resist Don Juan — what they cannot resist is the lure of a 'catch', of making an excellent match, for Don Juan is the scion of one of the country's leading noble families. What was then called seduction would today be termed 'breach of promise'.

The victims of the original Don Juan were disappointed not so much in love as in their hopes: they were not able to marry a Spanish aristocrat. Don Juan's sin was not, for the dramatist and his age, that he broke women's hearts but that he cynically broke his vows, flouted his promises, made a mockery of the sanctity of marriage, and failed to pay due respect even to a man he had himself killed, inviting his victim's statue to dine with him. His actions defied the sacred laws of religion and were a denial of God. That is why at the end of the play he is smitten by the wrath of Heaven and descends into the realm of the damned. When the statue shakes his hand Don Juan bursts into flame and crumples in a heap.

There is little about women's broken hearts. Seventeenth-century Spaniards still observed that medieval chivalric convention whereby it is only the man who is supposed to find the woman appealing and not vice versa; the woman merely accepts or, at most, reciprocates the man's love. And it seems she reciprocates it only when she sees that this is to her practical advantage.

The transformation of this concept goes hand in hand with the transformation of the story of Don Juan in his subsequent incarnations. In Molière's play Don Juan is still a cynical troth-breaker — *un épouseur à toutes mains*, as his valet Sganarelle calls him — but in this case the betrayed woman's suffering plays a greater role: Don Juan's first wife, Donna Elvire, whom the knight has helped escape from a convent, returns in the play's most moving scene and urges Don Juan, whom she still loves, to repent.

But Don Juan becomes Don Juan in the sense we know him today only in Byron's verse novel. Here we are at the beginning of the nineteenth century, in the golden age of Romantic emotion. Love is now no longer a wild passion of the body, nor even a tender prelude to marriage, but an overwhelming feeling whose glorious prodigality suffuses every cranny of the soul. Byron's Don Juan is fated to arouse the love of every woman he meets — this saves his life in the course of his perilous escapades; when he is captured and enslaved, for example, he melts an oriental princess's heart.

From here it is but a short step to the modern antithesis of Don Juan, Shaw's John Tanner (the English form of Don Juan Tenorio) in *Man and Superman*. Here Shaw is determined to prove the poets of old quite wrong: it is always the woman who makes the first move, woman is the temptress. In vain does Don Juan flee from her to the deserts of Spain and the nether world; woman always catches up with him and, in the end, marries him.

Reading the old Spanish play I made another astonishing discovery. Don Juan is shipwrecked and the sea casts him ashore. When he comes to his senses, he finds himself being tended by a fishergirl. Don Juan opens his eyes — and, just as he is, drenched through and through, he immediately falls in love, declaring his love for the girl on the spot. I believe that this is still the essential secret of every Don Juan. This is the lesson to be drawn from the memoirs of that greatest practising Don Juan of all, Casanova.

For someone to be a Don Juan, the essential condition is not that every woman should fall under his spell, but that he should fall under the spell of every woman.

Someone who is choosy cannot be a Don Juan, as he has to be able — immediately, fatally, unconditionally — to fall in love with each and every woman, as if she were the very first to have stirred his heart. His past, all his previous women, must melt away — a Don Juan is without memory, and he may not think ahead — a Don Juan has no imagination: his whole being is focused on the present moment, the particular amorous adventure. Because a convincing liar needs to believe in his own lies. This is a necessary element in the psychology of that timeless human archetype: the philanderer.

Notes to Chapter 5

1. [First published *Új idők*, 4 (21 January 1940).]
2. [The play was first published about 1630.]

PART II

Essays on Modernism

CHAPTER 6

Stefan George (1926)[1]

I.

Stefan George's artistic career resembled that of all who in our time instil words
with new meanings, and whose new content necessarily involves dismantling old
forms and creating new ones — a view not universally accepted. Some found
George incomprehensible; others, content to label him 'a decadent' and 'an
aesthete', passed him over without probing his work more deeply. In particular, he
was accused of setting himself apart, arrogantly withdrawing from everyday life
and the issues confronting nineteenth-century society. Gradually, however, the new
rhythms brought forth and preserved in his splendid isolation found their way to
ears destined to hear them, the initially enclosed circle continued to expand, and
now George is seen as one of the figures who have imbued their nation with self-
confidence and pride. The shocks of the Great War opened deaf ears to much that
was previously obscure in George's work and made it clear, and George has himself
played an outstanding role in the postwar cultural renaissance.

   This study is not intended to offer a complete cross-section of George's thought.
The paragraphs that follow try merely to justify — and in a not entirely consistent
manner at that — the single claim that with Stefan George the history of the
German spirit entered a new phase, and that this development was at the same time
a return to certain ancestral embodiments of the German spirit, way of life, and
vision that we are wont to refer to globally as the Middle Ages. For in George's
veins, despite his modernity and qualification to represent his time, there flows the
blood of the Wolframs, the Walters, and the Gottfrieds, and he himself resumes the
path at the point where Martin Luther deviated from it. He is the first German poet
since the Reformation whose work is not contingent on Lutheranism and its more
distant descendants, Romanticism and German philosophy.

   A claim in such negative terms is impossibly vast and difficult to sustain.
For virtually everything German cannot but denote Lutheran, starting with
the language, New High German, which wears Luther's features via German
scholarship and was in effect launched by Luther's critique, and continuing by
way of German philosophy, constructed upon the Lutherist freedom principle,
ultimately to embrace German poetry in the 'individual-only' spirit, and German
religious life, expressed in the Lutheran-style sanctity of the subjective religious
experience — indeed, virtually everything. George was largely unaffected by all of
this and shaped the language to his own perspective almost as energetically as had

Luther in his time, and continued along the German spiritual track that the great Catholic German mystics had abandoned in the fourteenth century, paving the way for the Reformation and giving the initial impetus to the German individualism subsequently to stamp its mark, to a certain extent, on the whole of Europe.

In contrast, George is not an *individualist* in the nineteenth-century sense of the word. He does not claim that every distinctive individual experience, not even the most profound ones, if they happen to be 'individual-only', represent a value; it is not the aim of his poetry — or at least not the primary one — to offer a faithful mirror of his individuality. His individuality is supra-individual and only through its sharing of objective values does it gain that *Weihe* so important for him, the justification that alone entitles him to record his life: because it is precisely through this that his life has ceased to be 'individual-only', 'one-off', and achieved universal validity as the human vehicle of the eternal.

This negative claim is at the same time a positive one. George is not an *individualist*: an individualist is in actual fact a part of the whole that has achieved autonomy, and in breaking away from the Whole has lost awareness of it. This is why German poetry is a poetry of loneliness: the autonomous element, the Ego, being insufficient unto itself, yearns eternally for the romanticized Other, the not-Ego, that is to say, for the Whole. This yearning is the keynote of modern German poetry, the root of all German Sentimentalism (= the ache resulting from the loneliness of the Ego), of Romanticism (= the longing for a synthesis with the not-Ego), and of *Weltschmerz* (= the sense of bitterness resulting from the impossibility of achieving such a synthesis). By contrast, George is not lonely (discounting certain unavoidable turning points in his life, which recur almost with the regularity of solar eclipses); he feels he is part of the Whole that exists for him and can be seen from within and is habitable terrain; he is in and of the cosmos, the ordered, 'furnished' universe. He feels that he is moved by the same laws as move the stars, and conversely: the stars, too, are moved by the laws that govern him, not because he possesses in his consciousness a microcosm of that which forms the macrocosm, but vice versa: because in the macrocosm is incorporated his own microcosm, which is like the macrocosm in that it is unitary.

2.

The poet confronts the world and reacts to what he encounters; this reaction is poetry. The reaction may take a variety of forms. Some poets are emotional lyricists, for example Sándor Petőfi, recording feelings that things stir up in them; some are reflective poets, for example Imre Madách, registering their thoughts about things; yet others are solemn and lofty poets, for example Mihály Vörösmarty, concerned with the principles of how to direct things. The poets who stand on poetry's highest rung are those *through whom* it is the things themselves that speak, for example János Arany, and of whom we are wont to say that they describe things as they really are.

Except that to see things as they really are belongs to God alone, as only in Him exists from all eternity the essence of each and every thing. We view them only as they *seem*, every single person differently moreover, just as a beam of light will strike each person's eyes differently. We can at most get within striking distance of things as they are, by means of the chance intuitions of some mysterious clairvoyance belonging to and bestowed on us by love. This is why the great creative artist is the master craftsman of love: his love being greater, he sees things more accurately. A great poet can be said to be objective if it is at least his intention to try to express not his own subjective thoughts and feelings about things, but the essence of things themselves, since of course things are, in their essence, objective. He is, at the same time, also subjective, in that humans are finite and each person's vision is coloured by his personality. This duality, of objective things and subjective vision, is what lends poetry its enchantment, proceeding as it does simultaneously from within and from without, and creating through the magic of language a synthesis between the Ego and the Not-Ego.

What, therefore, a great poet expresses in his poem is neither the whole wide world, nor the poet's microcosm, but both at once: the poet's world vision is differentiated from all other acts of perception in that, in his work, subject (the viewer), object (what the viewer views), and predicate (the act of viewing) are one and the same, and in the world that he sees the poet has already included himself, and the world, through this action, views its own self. We have said *world vision* and not *world view*, as in present-day parlance world view tends to refer to the entirety of a person's views, opinions, and axioms arranged any old how, and not the primordial elemental *unity of vision* that characterizes the poet. All of us have, or at least ought to have, a world view, whereas only to a chosen few creative artists is it granted to objectivize, project, and immortalize their vision of the world, in short, to portray the world.

In what follows we shall therefore be looking at George's world vision transformed into poetry. We shall not be examining George's thoughts, feelings, attitudes, or principles, but things as George sees them. Clearly, then, it will not be possible to distil into the form of words, judgements, or notions elements that are pictorial and not abstractions. As George so deftly put it when writing about his work: 'And never for the many nor through speech | It comes incarnate rarely to the rare'.[2]

The poet's world vision manifests itself in his work in two ways: in terms of substance and of form. In terms of substance: what the poet sees, what remains essential and to be expressed once the world has been filtered through his personality is for the poet to select. In terms of form: how the poet sees, as the seeing mode specific to his poetry is also evident in its 'how', and in George, the laws of vision and creation being the same, this is a question of poetic technique.

George's poetic technique, his 'how', is itself an innovation vis-à-vis the poetry of the nineteenth and twentieth centuries, a return to an earlier poetic approach that was dying out in the German lyric. German poetry since Goethe was that of the one-off experience, in line with Goethe's principle that all lyric was occasional poetry. The poet's technique is to delineate whatever the inspiration of the moment presented to him; it may be that the next moment will contain a totally contrary experience, in which case he will unselectively delineate whatever and how much that moment serves up. His gestures are first to open his eyes wide, then shut them immediately, and provide an account of what he has seen. This technique culminated in the Impressionist lyric of the late nineteenth century, when the poet no longer embraced anything lasting or showed any reaction to experience, but merely mirrored whatever passed before him: at the mercy of mood he was a cradle rocked by an unknown hand or a windblown leaf, as Verlaine characteristically put it. This poetic treatment flows organically from the Lutheran, individualist vision of the world: the process began when the Church split up into separate believers, then society into individuals, individuals into experiences, then space into locations, and time into moments — so what else can the poet do but express the point in space and time? The expression of a world viewed and lived in the form of atoms can only be atomized poetry, as reinforced by modern determinism, whereby the poet does not even believe he has any way of controlling the experiences and moments flitting past and becomes passively addicted to his own vision.

George is not a poet of the one-off experience. He is *permanent* and it might almost be said that what he records is experience as an a priori: as they process before him the images change but the background against which they appear does not. Nor is his standpoint vis-à-vis the object the conditioned attitude of enslavement: he is more like a general, mustering his troops in serried ranks according to a preordained plan. It is the content of moments that he, too, offers, as lyric poetry can deal only in moments of time (continuous duration requires the epic), but these are not in their content one-off, sudden, unexpected, and unpredictable, like the relativized impressionistic moment: in his case the experience and the moment make actual something that was already and still is permanently there in potential. The experience of the moment exists not for its own sake but only as a part of the empathetic Experience of the Whole, just as his own self is part of the cosmos as a whole. It is this permanence of his vision that Friedrich Gundolf suggestively calls *Dauerblick*.

Naturally this manner is manifest not only in George's attitude to experience but also in the form of his poems: rhythm, structure, metaphor, and image alike. For it is the poetic form that helps us understand the 'how' of the poet's world vision and makes us experience it through his eyes.

Permanency in George's images takes the form of *plasticity*. George's images and similes are calm, static, and viewable in the round, like carvings. This too is a rather unique phenomenon in German lyric poetry. The young Goethe, in whom perhaps German individualism first turned into poetry, broke with the two-dimensional images of traditional verse and fused into a single image impressions from different domains of feeling and replaced static with moving images. While Goethe himself did subsequently achieve that plasticity without which a truly great poet is unimaginable, his acolytes took as their starting point the lyrical poetry of his youth: the German Romantics, and their successors in world literature, the French and Frenchified Symbolists, who later carried to the extreme the disintegrative process whereby clean lines were replaced by fuzzy blobs of colour creating images that are not representational but impressionistic, trying after an overall impression of the chaotic merging of every domain of feeling, definitively sidelining plasticity and yielding to a music-like undulation or rocking motion — in short, atmosphere became autonomous.

George's formative force is akin to and shares its roots with his plasticity: his every poem is constructed with an almost stark rigour, without redundancy or impediment, and with a plasticity of inner structure. This rigidity is again in contrast with the impressionistic lyric, which deliberately avoids formal composition and reflects colours in the chaotic sequence they are proffered by life. It is never possible at the beginning to know how a poem will end.

George's incomparable creative power is evident not only in the individual poem. Poems are clustered into complete, closed verse-cycles complementing each other in a structured manner in each individual volume. To go a step further: George's entire *oeuvre* can be viewed as if constructed according to a unitary plan, with each poem having its own place and every poem in its proper place. Thus George's *oeuvre*, derived instinctively from George's 'ordered' nature, becomes an image and a projection of the great Hierarchy. If we wished to characterize George by a single attribute, we could justly call him the 'poet of order'. This is what makes him stand out sharply from those chaotic, eternally immature, 'freewheeling' individualists.

3.

In the material and essence of George's world image, the elements of two worlds are intermingled: those of Catholic Christianity and Antiquity. He himself perceives these, the antique and the Christian spirit, as a priori the two most powerful driving forces of humanity, necessarily presupposing and complementing each other. In his verse-cycle *Standbilder*, he shows in static images, as if statues of gods, the forces that direct the human spirit. One single poem — the first — encapsulates a still shot of Antiquity and Christianity, as if symbolizing that the two are primary and indivisible. George, too, is one of those who want to build a 'third Reich', a 'new Church', or call it what you will, based on a synthesis of the spirit of Antiquity and Christianity.

In examining his vision of the world, we will first focus on his vision of nature, the theme of his volume entitled *Das Jahr des Seele*. It should be said at once that George's vision of nature is *not sentimental*. The essence of the sentimental view of nature, historically deriving from the Calvinist Rousseau, is a longing for nature on the part of humans who have become cut off from it. Later, as that longing adulterates and falsely idealizes the image of nature the sentimentalist proceeds to dress it up in all the colours missing from his life. This sentimental vision of nature is a further consequence of individualism, which has wrenched the individual from nature in its entirety, and is a variety of *sich fliehen*, the flight from the self, to which the individual, having fallen into the bottomless pit of loneliness, is compelled to resort. In the case of those who nevertheless managed to connect with nature, it was their overflowing *Lebensgefühl*, which suddenly and violently burst the dam of the self, that provided them with a link to it: they, like the young Goethe and Hölderlin, became pantheists. That is to say, the experience of nature came at the expense either of nature or of the Self undergoing the experience.

In George's lyrical poetry nature is the vehicle not of yearning but of life itself: it is the mother earth from which all life — physical and mental — springs, *die grosse*

Nährerin. George does not feel disconnected from nature, just as he does not feel he is of one essence with it in the manner of the pantheists. He feels part of the Whole, of which nature is also a part, and only a part, and not the pantheists' 'all'. He is aware that he, too, is governed by those superhuman and supernatural laws that rule nature, and that their internal rhythms are one and the same. This already finds expression in the title of his volume *Das Jahr des Seele.* The year is the symbol of nature's eternal law — here the year is at the same time the year of the soul, since the laws of nature and the Self are intertwined. This is also evinced in the volume's internal structure, particularly the first cycle, which is divided into three sections: each soul-state corresponds to one of nature's seasons and in the poems the two meld inseparably together. The sequence *Nach der Lese* is autumn and mature love that knows in advance that it will end; *Waller im Schnee* is winter and love that has died; *Sieg des Sommers* is at the same time the triumph of love, a fulfilment that can progress no further. In these poems the imagery of nature and soul coincide exactly: the soul's situation is possible only in this particular setting and the setting only acquires any sustainable human meaning by reason of the soul's situation; nature is like the soul and the soul is like nature. The structure of these poems recalls that of Hungarian folksong but while in the folksong nature and soul are parallel, in George they intersect.

The volume *Das Jahr des Seele,* and the other poems of George offering his vision of nature, are all permeated by a certain muted, looming, one might say incurable brooding. The joyful sense of nature that is the keynote of the young Goethe or Hölderlin is virtually unknown to George, as in him the vision of nature is always accompanied by some dull ache, and this ache is somehow so all-pervasive and unutterable that it ceases to be personal and is independent of any personal distress of his own. This pain resides in nature itself, things speak to us of George's pain, the pain of things, that great impersonal suffering familiar to everyone for whom nature has been transformed into experience. This is not by any means the nineteenth century's *Weltschmerz* (= pain because of the world), but the world's pain (= pain for the world).

4.

Stefan George's historical vision is *not evolutionist*: he does not believe that humanity is gradually changing for the better and progressing towards some humanly determinable goal, according to which ours is potentially the best of all possible worlds. Evolutionism, too, is a consequence of the *sich fliehen*: those who sought the meaning of their own lives outside of themselves, in some appointed goal, whether it be, as in the case of Rousseau and most recently Tolstoy, in the rediscovery of nature, or through a history-based *Bildungsideal,* like the German classics, or as in the second half of the nineteenth century in less elevated and more prosaic things which projected that aim onto humankind and its entire history.

George is well aware that every age exists for and of itself (disregarding its ultimate meaning) and not so as to pave the way for the next and the following ages; each age contains within itself its own meaning and purpose and also a self-judgement, depending on how far it is able to realize itself. He does not see history as progressing in a straight line, but as an undulation: there are ages in which we are close to the goals that lie within us, the quality of the divine implanted in humankind, and there are low periods, that have lost their faith and themselves. And the perihelion, proximity to God, is the sole measure of the ages — all the other evolutionist criteria, such as culture, the common weal, beneficence, Hegelian *Freiheit*, are but the projection onto history of our age's longing for transitory values and human beings' fanciful interpretations of superhuman events.

Because of this historical vision of his, it is naturally to be expected that George has clear views on the pre-eminent age of Catholicism, the Middle Ages, and he is the one who rehabilitates the Middle Ages in art. At first glance it may seem audacious to suggest that he should be the one to rehabilitate the German Middle Ages. Especially to us Hungarians it may appear curious, because our national epic, the most powerful portrayal of the Hungarian ethnos in the nineteenth century, János Arany's *Toldi* trilogy, succeeds in conferring reality on both what is timelessly Hungarian and characteristically medieval, without deficiencies or falsifications. But we must not forget that the difference between the Hungarian Middle Ages and contemporary Hungary is much less than, for example, between the German Middle Ages and contemporary Germany, as the essence of the Hungarian people is far less in evidence in the area where historical mutations primarily take place — the cultural and social level — than in the case of the German people. Hungarian everyday life as such (and as Hungarian identity is involved, this alone is the essential issue) was not very different in the Middle Ages from how it is today, only the means of its implementation have changed.

On the other hand this claim might seem contradictory because it is well-known that the rehabilitation of the Middle Ages in German literature had already begun with Goethe's *Götz von Berlichingen*, one of the programmatic works of the German Romantic movement. Nor has interest in the Middle Ages waned since then; indeed, a degree of ruined-castle sentimentalism is part and parcel of all German life. The Romantics did indeed manage to wash the epithet 'dark' off the label attached to the Middle Ages by ahistorical Enlightenment and rationalism. However, it now became necessary to cleanse the period of the Romantics' no less unjustifiable fantastic imagery, the topos of the *mondbeglänzte Zaubernacht*. For the Romantics falsified the Middle Ages just as much as they did nature. For them the Middle Ages, too, became a matter of *sich fliehen*, providing them with a place to hide from themselves or their age and its concomitant tasks. As in the case of nature, they clothed the Middle Ages with the embellishments produced by their abundant imagination and sought in vain amid the nineteenth century's drab grey bourgeoisie. And thus came into being the Romantic Middle Ages, with its anaemic minstrel knights, dull lords of the castle, fair maidens shrouded in chiffon, and its rattling tinpot weapons and Madonna-less Madonna cult. Hungarian literature, too, is not untouched by this vision of the Middle Ages, perceptible in the work of the two Kisfaludys, Jósika, and even Jókai. For the epigone literature of the mid-nineteenth century the Middle Ages provided a well-stocked museum from which it was always possible to snatch a rusty sword or dusty tale (see, for example, von

Scheffel's *Ekkehard*, 1855). For the 'neo-Romantics' like Heinrich and Julius Hart, Eduard Stucken, and Karl Vollmoeller it provided a decorative backdrop, something exotic with nothing homespun about it, against which to play out their thoroughly modern tales.

George's Middle Ages, as revealed in his *Bücher der Sagen und Sänge*, is not that of the Romantics. It is not that perfect kingdom in which yearning finds refuge, so gratifying to bewail and whose irrecoverability makes it preferable to give up on any attempt to influence one's own times. George knows full well that no one today can turn into medieval man, because in every age the human face of eternal Truth is different. He also appreciates that feature of the Middle Ages with which the Romantics most closely identified: the unending, gnawing yearning that suffused the medieval soul. He knows, however, that this is not the Romantics' aimless, disembodied, hopeless longing 'ins Blaue', but a wholly concrete longing for the East and the Holy Sepulchre, the flesh-and-blood Noble Lady, medieval man's concrete, physical Heaven: the yearning that produced crusader armies, knights, and saints, and not dreamers and artists.

George's historical vision delineates not only past ages but also his and our own, as in the verse-cycle *Zeitgedichte* in his volume *Der siebente Ring*. The *Zeitgedichte* are odes in praise of eternal values that have survived into, or been renewed in, the present age and are addressed to people or objects who or which stand out prominently, in sharp contours, against the age in its entirety and flooded with such radiance that the darkness surrounding them, the age, is all the more sepulchral as a result. From a person who measures the value of any age by its nearness to God we can hardly expect anything less than that he should see the age in which we live in the sombrest of colours.

With stunning, terrifying words he lambasts the age whose ideas have become dead abstractions, whose blood has been drained, that pursues means instead of ends, pleasures instead of beauty, that has cheapened every virtue, in which purity has become a lick and a promise, kindness has been replaced by charity, humility by unassumingness, respect by mannerliness, seriousness by reliability, wisdom by sagacity... He despises the dead and stunted age that goes hurtling off in a thousand directions and has a thousand kinds of worries because it has lost the essential One, an age that has gone farther from God than any before. In one of the finest poems in the *Zeitgedichte* cycle, *Die tote Stadt*, George introduces to us the dark vision of the Ancient City atop a cliff, sunken in poverty and glowering blackly on high, while at its foot teem the people of the New City built in the bay, chasing after material goods and growing richer by the day. But the Ancient City stands serene amidst its fading grandeur, secure in the knowledge that there will come a time when the people of the New City will make their way up the cliff in tearful procession, saying: 'A barren pain is blighting us, we sicken | [...] and unless you help, we die.'[3]

And it will then be the turn of the Ancient City to pass judgement and decline.

This image is quite startling: no nineteenth-century pessimistic poet viewed his age more darkly than George. But with this difference, that George is no pessimist; the cosmic law-bearer does not lack hope, he is not despairing, and does not revel in universal destruction like the master craftsmen of decadence, and certainly does not use the law to exculpate himself for his failings in the manner of the Expressionists, those chaotic, songless sons of 'an accursed, chaotic, songless century'. George acclaims the values which the age has preserved, the forces that can lead to its rebirth, as well as the ideas in whose spirit he thinks it must be reborn.

5.

We come now to George's vision of the Idea. This too is a vision, just like his vision of history and nature, and is not to be considered as thought or speculation. It is the word *vates*, translated into Hungarian during the language renewal movement as *látnok*, 'seer', that best expresses the great poet's attitude to the world of ideas: as for Truth, it is what the philosopher thinks, the enthusiast feels, and the artist sees.

Truth is one and timeless, but no human can grasp it in its entirety and its core remains forever hidden. What we perceive as truth is always only a detail of the 'One Truth' and looks as it does only from a particular viewpoint. As with every individual, so every age, too, sees Truth from a different angle, in varying degree and depth, hence the need for each age to have both its own *vates* through whose eyes each generation learns to see, and its own creative artist to immortalize the vision and endow it with form and reality, and thereby also to immortalize the age, because the most profound content of the age consists in what it sees of Truth and how it sees it.

George expounded his vision of Truth in three of his most mature works: *Teppich des Lebens*, where it is indeed a vision, *Siebente Ring,* where it takes the form of lived reality, and in his volume *Stern des Bundes*, where it is embodied as dogma.

Stefan George is the poet of Order. The world exists for him as the vehicle and embodiment of eternal laws, as a cosmos: in equal measure nature and history, and traversed by the stars and by human life. Each human being has his own law: his worth depends on how far he obeys it. This law does not take the form of written words, it is not some bundle of moral axioms, but a law that lives within us, flesh of our flesh, blood of our blood, the meaning, essence, *eidos*, and purpose of the individual human life. George's law was embodied in the Angel of the *Vorspiel*, one of the most sublime visions in world literature, and subsequently his life's work consisted solely in living and articulating the law set forth by the Angel. 'But now a blessed spirit holds the scales, | Now I am governed by the angel's will'.[4]

This obedience, this everlasting dutifulness in the spirit of the law is what lends George's poetry its distinctive gravitas and pathos, its *Weihe*; it is as if every poem of his were saying 'I am writing this not because this is how I experienced it and saw it and did not want it to sink without trace — I am writing it because this is how it was meant to be, I am a poet at the behest of a higher power, even if it is not my will'. For George his calling meant a burdensome asceticism, distancing himself from everything foreign and extraneous, all that was outward-looking and at variance, thereby disrupting the poet's immense and stubbornly maintained concentration. Many of his poems stress how difficult it is to bear the weight of his law and how often he is on the verge of buckling, like St Christopher the ferryman, under his sublime burden.

Yet the heavy burden of the laws of his calling is visited not only upon the chosen poet; the law of which he has become aware is at the same time that of Everyman, located as it is in the deeper-most recesses of our Selfhood, whence the song of the *vates* bursts forth. This law is simultaneously the most individual and the most general, for those are the regions inhabited by the supra-individual, the Eternal that resides in man. The most important virtue humanity possesses is respect for the law. Moral law and respect for it are delineated in the fourth of the *Standbilder*:

> When firm and grave she comes to us today
> With ruthless eyes, we do not shirk her call,
> For now we niche her in the marble hall
> And bend before her noble will and pray.[5]

And it is precisely in this voluntary bowing to noble duress that our jealously guarded treasure, freedom, is manifest, so that when the disorganized, chaotic powers present within the world and ourselves urge us to revolt, we can be free of our heredity and evil circumstances and freely submit to the law. The truly free do not consider the law in terms of blind fate or ill-will inimical to themselves, but deem it *noble*. This, then, is how the problem of the contradiction between fate and free will is resolved: in freedom we go to meet our fate, joyfully and with dignity obeying the command, which is ineluctable. George is not a determinist. Yes, indeed, it ought to be up to ourselves to take a stand against fate in intention and with our inner being, and to rise up against the law, as did so many nineteenth-century pessimists: this rising up against the eternal lies at the root of all the bitter resentment on the part of the everlastingly harassed everlasting rebels. George repeatedly counsels against such a rebellion, as there is greater freedom to be had when we bend the knee to noble coercion.

Within us are contained the law, the resolve for its fulfilment, and jurisdiction over ourselves. Everything is to be sought within ourselves: this is another of George's cardinal tenets, '*alles seid ihr selbst und drinne*'. He is uncompromising in his condemnation of every kind of Romantic *sich fliehen*, be it to faraway lands or far-off days, other people, abstract thought and especially enthralment (adopting Hölderlin's collocation *heilig nüchtern*), oblivion:

> You ride in headlong haste and have no goal,
> You ride, a whirlwind, over sea and land,
> You ride through men and yearn for one to bind you
> Who can never be bound, for one to fill you
> Who can never be filled, and shun a peace
> Where no one will confront you but yourself
> From whom you flinch as from your foulest foe,
> And your escape? The death you deal yourselves.[6]

By 'our self' is meant not any state of mind that can be conceptualized, exteriorized, or viewed from the outside, nor the soul in any psychological sense, as that again is just *sich fliehen*, whereby the soul beholds itself as some third person, something 'other', wandering off on the labyrinthine paths of its spiritual life and revelling in its own exuberance: an exuberance ultimately a miscellany of extraneous stray items — impressions, memories, phantasms — and in so doing again loses sight of its ultimate selfhood, which by this time really is 'our self', without any path inwards or outwards. This self, to which George urges us to return, is beyond concept or feeling and defies further analysis: it is our metaphysical ego, the earthly vehicle of things eternal, the bedrock of all religious life.

The return to oneself is George's most significant novum as regards German literature, which even from the purely literary historical angle and disregarding its ideological background, subsists in the spirit of *sich fliehen*: in translations, transpositions, pastiches; and neglectful of its own German identity, goes chasing after the major alien forms, feels at home in an alien milieu, in the exotic, the past, in fantasy. The greatest of the Romantics did get so far as to appreciate George's lesson as the height of sagacity: Novalis — perhaps unconsciously — in his story of *Hyazinth und Rosenblüte*, where a young man sets off to see the world and, his goal achieved, lifts the veil of the mysterious Goddess only to recognize that this is the girl he had left back home. Or Hegel's triadic rhythm, where via antithesis the spirit achieves synthesis with the recognition that what it is confronting is also his own self. This sagacity, this synthesis were for George a given already.

But it is not only in the world of the spirit that the *sich fliehen* ceases to exist, it needs to do so in space and time also, in the *hic et nunc* licensed afresh by our fresh discovery of our self. This discovery of the self involves an incalculable intensification of life and its reality, life of a sort lived purely and simply and experiencing neither periods of stagnation nor dark nights of the soul, but continually and permanently suffused with the sense of its ultimate selfhood, the tranquil intoxication of the *Hochgefühl*. Of this life that has found itself the Angel of the *Vorspiel* says: 'Dispatched to you by radiant Life I come, | An envoy'.[7]

In terms of the time this means that George breaks with the Romantics' sponging off memory and the evolutionists' cult of the future and of hope. These are both examples of *sich fliehen*; for George it is first and foremost the moment in which he is present that matters, this is the moment he wants to inhabit totally, looking neither forward nor back: 'Und was ihr heut nicht leben könnt, wird nie' ('And what you cannot grasp today can never be').[8] This is not, of course, that chance moment of the Impressionist, no sooner here than gone. George's moment is that afforded by fate and the law, whose function it is to be the vehicle of things eternal and to create a bridge from the moment to an eternal from whose depths the moment is in turn infused with radiance, just as on the surface of even the smallest lake there is room for both the sun and the moon. And this applies during every single moment, as human acceptance of things eternal is not to be deferred to some vague time just around the corner — and thus the moment is no longer fleeting but eternal. The paradox of that eternal moment that brings death to Protestantism's pre-eminent exponent of it, eternity-seeking Faust, is for the eternity-finding Catholic Stefan George a precondition of existence.

The life of a human being living those eternal moments gains a wonderful concreteness. The moment — the really present — unencumbered by past or future, its contours not blurred, whether through comparison or commingling, by things not belonging to it, reveals things as they truly are. Such a person's life becomes marvellously coordinated and self-contained, as what in another is diffracted into a thousand longings and memories, here gathers to a single focal point and that life, in Walter Pater's apt phrase, always 'burns with a hard, gem-like flame'. When we switch off all that is non-present, the advantage we gain is beyond all measure, and we become, via the totality of the things present, more searching, and by virtue of the great paradox inherent in all forgoing find that what we forgo we get back a hundredfold because only through the act of forgoing it is it possible for us to appreciate what we have forgone. Concreteness is in fact beyond description, since its cardinal characteristic is that it is not analyzable; for the man of concreteness, everything is what it is.

The present offers a perspective in which the Ancient and Catholic worlds meet. What distinguishes most markedly those who lived in Antiquity and the Middle Ages from the present-day person of culture is the fact that the former were present in that moment and while they were living it simultaneously experienced things eternal just as concretely as any person or thing. Today's *Kulturmensch*, on the other hand, inhabits an intellectual and emotional plane not his own and is attached to things by transient feelings and thoughts. Such people do not have a life of their own, only a secondhand existence, their actions motivated by convention and cultural schemata; the overestimation of cultural values has warped their view of life. Those who belong to today's 'pragmatic' world have no feel for things as they actually are.

And with this we come to the core of George's world vision: George, the new poet of the present, does away with *sich fliehen* in the world of space also, and seeks within space and our selves a new endorsement relative to *the body*. Not, of course, merely the material body, that driven by material instincts, but the imperishable body, the temple of the Holy Spirit. This is the ultimate meaning of the present and is where Antiquity and medieval Catholicism achieve synthesis. The Ancient World respected the body because it perceived in corporeal beauty the reflection of the beauty of the fundamental Idea, since the infinite perspective of physical beauty led to things eternal. The Middle Ages respected the body, the soul's faithful partner, because the Word was made flesh and because through Christ's Ascension the body, too, was sanctified. It was from respect, and not denial, of the body that the flesh-mortifying asceticism of the Middle Ages also sprang: precisely because people respected the body they strove to mould it, cleanse it of its base and material urges, to make it pliant and compliant, so that it might be the worthy vehicle of the soul; it was by making it a slave to the soul that they set the body free — free from materiality and the Foe. Even the Latin mystics, those flesh-subjugating champions of the soul, had respect for the body: for celestial beauty in bodily form, the Madonna that dwelt in their visions, doctrinal faith (= the concrete form of inner faith), the body's outward acts of piety, poverty (= the most perfect mode of corporeal existence), the miracles, the visions, the stigmata (= the manifestation of the supernatural over the dominion of nature and the body), and above all the Eucharist (the flesh-and-blood Godhead that dwells among us). The great German mystics were the first to start denying the body (and not just verbally: that had been done before them, but always, however, in terms of perishable flesh). Meister Eckhart and his followers zealously subordinated visions, stigmata, dogmatic faith, outward acts, and quality of life to the only matter they deemed important: inner experience, whereby it was in spirit that Christ was born again in them. Thus began the German mind's cult of 'soul-only', 'spirit-only'. What had for the Gottesfreunde still been just a distinctive nuance within the bosom of the Church, had led Luther and the reformers into heresy:[9] they jettisoned dogma, good works, sacraments, the saints (= the embodied vehicles of Truth), the Church hierarchy (the earthly mirror of eternal order), and removed the body from the Eucharist making it purely symbolic for the sake of the 'soul-only' faith factor. Once embarked on the path of disembodiment, there was no stopping. Lutheranism as a religion led on the one hand to the sickly, anaemic mysticism of the Pietists and the Moravian Brethren that derived from it, culminating in the sentimental hypertrophy of the soul, and on the other hand to the wholly abstract, speculative 'convictions' of enlightened, liberal Protestantism, which later broke away from religion and gave rise to German idealism, that most abstract, unrealistic, and life-denying manifestation of the human spirit. The Spirit, the Pure Ideal, achieved autonomy, sloughed off the body, abandoned the earth, and moved into the realm of the abstract — it was set free. But this freedom brought little recompense: in this dualism body and soul pined for each other like Plato's hermaphrodites.

By contrast what George proclaims are more or less literally the lessons of Plato's *Phaedrus* and *Symposium*. He himself summarizes the goal of the Templars (the guardians of the Idea) thus: *Den leib vergottet und den gott verleibt,* the liberation of the body by the ever-present Idea and the realization of the Idea by means of the body.

6.

The activity of the Artist, when his spell conjures immaterial Idea into matter — marble, paint, stone, or language — is the secular analogue of the priest's activity when the words of Consecration bring about the act of transubstantiation. It is this that gives the artist his enduring significance: he is the intermediary between Idea and humankind. In earthly terms he is the one through whom the Word is made flesh and dwells amongst us. George is one of the select few to have re-embodied ideas, spellbinding them into imperishable concrete forms, into the material of language.

In our time the significance of the great creative artist is perhaps even greater than is that of the exponent of the perfect life, because today the latter is able to influence only an isolated group, as most people have not eyes to perceive life's true values, whereas the artist will seek us out in the dimension whither we have fled to escape from ourselves, that of culture and works of art, and will beckon us back to life and Truth. An age of art is always one that the Idea is preparing to, or has already, abandoned: Greek drama was born when the Sophists had irrevocably undermined Greek faith, and the Middle Ages had already begun to decline when Dante erected an eternal monument to the spirit, which was on the verge of being lost forever. For appetite is aroused by dearth and what arouses the artist's desire and creative enthusiasm is that the Idea is no longer present. In periods that have lost their radiance, the untainted desire of the artist is alone capable of conjuring back the lost idea, through the magic of form that can raise the dead, and he alone can re-humanize it, endow it with bodily shape, and enable it to dwell amongst us.

Notes to Chapter 6

1. [First published in *Symposion*, 2 (1926).]
2. [Stefan George, 'Der Teppich', ll. 15–16, in *The Works of Stefan George*, trans. by Olga Marx and Ernst Morwitz, 2nd edn (Chapel Hill: University of North Carolina Press, 1974), p. 185 (hereafter cited as Marx and Morwitz) ('Sie wird den vielen nie und nie durch rede, | Sie wird den seltnen selten im gebilde').]
3. [George, *Die tote Stadt*, ll. 17–18, in Marx and Morwitz, p. 229 ('Uns mäht ein ödes weh und wir verderben, | Wenn ihn nicht helft').]
4. [George, *Vorspiel* III, ll. 3–4, in Marx and Morwitz, p. 170 ('Nun hält ein guter geist die rechte waage, | Nun tu ich alles, was der engel will'.]
5. [George, *Standbilder, das vierte*, ll, 1–4, in Marx and Morwitz, p. 196 ('Wenn heut sie naht mit würdig festem gange | Und strengem blick trifft sie nicht mehr enteiler, — | Ihr ist nun auch im marmorbau ein pfeiler | Und beter beugen wir uns edlem zwange').]
6. [George, *Der Stern des Bundes, Erstes Buch*, ll. 25–32, in Marx and Morwitz, pp. 326–27 ('Ihr fahrt in hitzigen tummel ohne ziel | Ihr fahrt im sturm, ihr fahrt durch see und land, | Fahrt durch die menschen … sehnt unfassbar ihr | Dass sie euch fassen … sehnt unfüllbar ihr | Dass sie euch füllen…und ihr scheut die rast | Wo ihr allein euch findet mit euch selbst | Bang vor euch selbst als eurem ärgsten feind | Und eure lösung ist durch euch der tod').]
7. [George, *Vorspiel* I, ll. 11–12, in Marx and Morwitz, p. 169 ('Das schöne leben sendet mich an dich, | Als beten').]
8. [George, *Der Stern des Bundes, Drittes Buch*, in Marx and Morwitz, p. 343.]
9. [Medieval lay mystical group within the Catholic church.]

CHAPTER 7

Ibsen (1928)[1]

A hundred years have passed since the birth of Ibsen. The European, indeed worldwide, celebration of the centenary finds that the 'Ibsen question' has been settled amicably: the most controversial literary issue of the end of the nineteenth and the beginning of the twentieth century has somehow been resolved, moreover, in the way that intellectual problems are generally resolved: not by anyone finding a solution to them but because in time they cease to be a problem.

It is therefore an opportune moment to review our attitude to Ibsen and examine what in the course of the great battles has been sloughed off and how much has withstood the ravages of the critical storm and remained as an objective value, perhaps to triumph in the coming centuries. What does Ibsen mean, without snobbery, as a living force, to the new generation that has grown up after the Ibsen wars and hence is the most competent to pass impartial judgement?

We had already encountered Ibsen at school, in the form of set texts, alongside the dramas of Sophocles and Shakespeare, as a representative, after Greek and courtly culture, of that third kingdom, the modern, but a modern that had already become a school text and therefore lost the elemental dynamism with which it had been charged. In our eyes Ibsen was already a classic, the classic that in terms of the age and in any case felt most close to us.

Because to us, to our enthusiastic high-school hearts, he did feel very close. I remember that on our trips up and down the Svábhegy, the hill on the outskirts of Budapest, we never tired of debating the meaning of the elusive symbol of one or other of his plays, and would boast of how many Ibsen plays we had read, in the same way that only a few years earlier we had bragged about our stamp collections or the number of goals we had scored. We became so familiar with Ibsen's distinctive style that eventually in every book we read the only thing that mattered was its symbols. I remember picking up a Jókai novel and being unable to understand it, because my Ibsen-besotted imagination discerned symbols everywhere but without being able to find the keys to them. This 'symbol-rage' dominated our lives like a never-ending parlour game, and with my closest friends we conversed in symbols.

But well beyond these games, Ibsen's life-forming influence on our generation was enormous. I mean truly life-affecting influence: I know of young men who, after mighty struggles with their soul, abandoned a career in the church for which they were training, drawing strength and consolation from Ibsen's dramas; I know of young marriages which resulted in extraordinary outcomes thanks to extensive reflection on the examples of *The Doll's House* and *The Lady from the Sea*. I think it could be shown statistically that Ibsen is one of those writers who, like Ady and Dostoevsky, had the greatest influence on the development of the young, in so far as literature can influence anything.

What gripped young people, us young people, was undoubtedly Ibsen's principal message: freedom. Perhaps this is the idea that all young people are most sensitive to; freedom is somehow one of the constituent driving principles of the young. But every age has its own concept of freedom, every generation demands freedom of a different kind. By freedom Ibsen in his youth understood political freedom, Norway's liberation, and democratic ideals; he wrote a drama about Cataline as well as a poem to the Hungarian freedom fighters of 1848. Later, however, he admitted that all these political freedoms are just freedoms and nothing compared with Freedom, the ideal, inner freedom of the individual. Politically he grew ever more conservative and from the social point of view he adopted the character of the buttoned-up aristocratic writer; but the freedom of the life of the soul hovered before him until the very last pieces that he wrote, like the snow-covered peaks his heroes wanted to scale even if it cost them their lives.

At first his conception of individual freedom was external, moralizing, and clamorous: in *The Doll's House*, for example, where it results in a serious quarrel between husband and wife and the wife's deserting her conjugal post. Later he became more and more refined, his concept of freedom becoming increasingly intimate and subtle: for the heroine of *The Lady from the Sea* freedom means only the freedom to choose. And Hedda Gabler commits suicide when she feels she has lost her inner freedom.

This ideal, of entirely internalized individual freedom, free of defiance and rebellion, was what the young found so pleasing. In our other favourites, the Russians and the French, literature presented the languid determinism of the *fin de siècle*, whereas from Ibsen there blew a more bracing wind towards us, the suggestion of individual freedom imbued us with the faith that we did, after all, possess free will, the ability to choose between good and evil (for Ibsen freedom was nothing other than Luther's *Freiheit eines Christenmenschen*: free will), and free we must be in the sense of the principle of responsibility in Ibsen; his masculine world of ideas was one of the first constructive forces that we imbibed from more recent literature; and for this reason, despite his many negative effects, Ibsen belongs among the benign masters.

But youth, too, passes and the nineteenth century, too, is long gone, and its foremost ideal, freedom, has also somehow frayed. Freedom is still the finest ideal-flower that has blossomed from the finest soil of Christian European culture; but after all our wars and revolutions there is no word that sticks more awkwardly in our throat, none that has been more abused, none that any man with a shred of decency employs with greater circumspection: he who has been bitten by a snake fears even a lizard. Who knows, if Petőfi were alive, perhaps he would have formulated the premiss of his famous quatrain about love and freedom otherwise.[2]

Ibsen's enthusiasm for freedom, too, which animated our youthful years, today seems to us somewhat alien, as if disconnected from life as it is lived, and at times it appears as supererogatory and unrealistic as his uncompromising 'either/or' heroes Brand, or Julian the Apostate, or Dr Stockmann, those belated representatives of the old, doctrinaire idealism, the last knights of the Marquis of Posa's, of Don Quixote's blood. When Ellida, the Lady from the Sea, demands of her husband the freedom to choose and then freely chooses him, the entire work, which is up to that point acutely profound psychologically, suddenly becomes mannered.

Today it is no longer the spirit of freedom that animates Ibsen's works; indeed, the fact that they endure in spite of this is evidence of their greatness. And along with Ibsen's concept of freedom now outmoded too are all those secondary problems and innovations in dramatic technique that were in his day seen as Ibsen's major achievements. (This tends to be very much the rule: in Byron and Heine, too, what has dated most is what their contemporaries adored or abhorred them for, and this will also be the fate of the Hungarian Endre Ady.)

The position of women, for example, one of Ibsen's major concerns, for which Strindberg mocked him as a bluestocking, has now ceased to be a problem for our souls; it is now natural that if a woman is also earning money she should be an equal-ranking member of a society like ours based on making money: what for Ibsen was a problem of the soul is today at most an economic issue and the framework for a variety of lesser problems, but ultimately something that goes without saying.

Similarly, the dramatic naturalism that Ibsen championed is today self-explanatory; indeed, it is rather passé and at odds with the latest trends. Today the expedients that Ibsen strove to eliminate from the drama — verse, the soliloquy, the aside, and the entire apparatus that raised the drama above the level of everyday life — all these are gradually regaining their respectability. Today's popular plays deploy with a casual naturalness the achievements for which Ibsen fought so hard: the middle-class dining room of Ibsen's plays has become the obligatory arena of the drama, and those on the front line of the new dramatic art are now making strenuous efforts to rid the stage of the whiff of the dining room. And talk of that much-vaunted double-speak — talking about something other than what we appear to be talking about — seems, after Maeterlinck, rather uncomfortable.

And, finally, as for Ibsen's most famous innovation, symbols: these are what have become most passé of all. When actors gradually realized that the wild duck was a symbol, they were overjoyed that they were performing a symbol and this term 'wild duck', they always acted creepily, in underlined italics, in capitals throughout, even in red capitals, thus emphasizing even more the contrived nature of the cliché-symbol. Eventually it began to feel comedic: what was all the fuss about this creature? Why does poor Solness need to climb to the top of the tower and break his neck, when it is, when all's said and done, a symbolic tower and it would be quite enough if he were to climb it symbolically and then at least he would not get killed.

Next, the critics proceeded to tear Ibsen limb from limb by showing how universal were mathematical forms in his work. It had to be granted that no one had constructed a dramatic composition with surer hands than he; no one better justified each entrance and exit; no one wrote more economically; no one laid the groundwork for the denouement with greater craftsmanship; no one managed to create dramatic tension more powerfully; and at the same time it had be admitted that precisely because of these towering achievements, he overegged his dramas just a fraction. Their perfection is on the verge of being detrimental to their realism; some small dramaturgical error would be such a relief in these impeccable compositions, because perhaps through such a flaw, such a gap, the wind of the untidiness and outrageousness of everyday life could blast some fresh air into their stuffy, formal world.

The more important Ibsen considers something, the less lifelike it becomes in his plays: it is what he wrote with his left hand that is most successful. His minor roles are bursting with life and genuine vision, yet his protagonists, though they may not be the incarnation of principles (were this the case he would not be an artist), are the embodiments of dramatic forces: at the moment of their birth the Tragic Muse leaning over their cradle so fashioned their souls that they fade away by the end of the fifth act; they are time-bombs. In the dialogues, too, those stretches that are intended to characterize canter smoothly along with a profound humour and unrivalled insight, while the great set-piece symbolic dialogues at times remind us of the verbal powwows of Indian chiefs determined to worm some great secret out of each other. What makes these dialogues sound artificial are both the continuous, ponderous repetitions and the apparent taking of the symbols literally. 'What do you want from that wild duck?' we would like cry out, 'for you know very well that the wild duck = the life lie; why don't you come right out with it?'

And then there are critics who claim that the wild duck is not, after all, a symbol but an allegory. This is not something that spells the end for the wild duck; for very great artists have employed allegory; indeed, the greatest writer's greatest work is one: the Divine Comedy. The allegory is very much a double-edged device: it can be used both to compose the most drily contrived of works and to allow us to come close to the greatest profundities that it is possible humanly to approach. It inheres in the distinctive nature of the resolution of the problem that the very element that most readily becomes obsolete in something intellectually new is that which bears within it most properties of the eternal. This also applies to Ibsen's symbols. But let this critique of symbols be now followed by an apologia for them.

Symbols as understood in Ibsen's time have become obsolete: their contents have become as obsolete as their technical significance in dramatic terms. But today we are beginning to appreciate these symbols in another sense, perhaps in the sense that Ibsen himself intended; at least, that is what the evidence of his letters suggests.

In these letters Ibsen is at pains to stress that he wants to depict only people and it is true that very many things that appear to be symbols or allegory are not in fact such, but should be understood literally, as they come from the mouth of the person that Ibsen makes them say them; they are not an allegory, but a pathological symptom. For example, Solness's susceptibility to dizzy spells should not be taken to mean that he has a sensitive conscience, but that he is susceptible to dizzy spells — that is what he is like. The fact that Ellida continually longs for the sea, the invigorating atmosphere of the coast, the endless play of colour upon the waves, does not mean that she longs for freedom; indeed, it is just this that it cannot mean because Ibsen has one of the characters in the play explain that it means a longing for the sea, the boundless complexity of the sea that preoccupies the mind of the hysterical woman.

One must bear in mind that Ibsen's characters, who speak and live in symbols, are not in fact simply the bourgeois diners in the bourgeois dining room, beings who operate on exactly the same level as our everyday life, from whose mouths the dramatist, for whatever reason, dangles 'speech-bubble' symbols. No: they are all of them eccentrics, all of them tainted by the faint shadow of madness. That they live among symbols is not due just to the calculating shrewdness of the playwright but the astonishingly accurate observations of someone who truly knows human beings. The findings of recent neurological research support that what appear to be Ibsen's allegories are depictions of reality. They have repeatedly shown that such things indeed exist, indeed are rather frequent: *every neurotic thinks in terms of symbols and inhabits a world of symbols.* Every neurotic symptom has in fact a symbolic meaning; it is just that the patient is unaware of it, too sick to divine that meaning. Let us take, for example, the appalling revulsion that neuropaths have to certain foods. Clearly this mass of affects, this rage, this repulsion or fear, does not pertain to the item of food, insignificant in itself, but to something that the food reminds the patient of, something it symbolizes.

Ibsen was drawn to pathological cases because he habitually depicted real human beings. Just as a doctor is able to examine more easily the structural features of an organ when it has hypertrophied, grown too large, so is the writer better able to examine some psychological aspect of a pathological case when that aspect has been isolated and has achieved distended and sickly dimensions. Great dramatists' heroes are always more or less pathological: Othello's jealousy is 'morbid', for example; or let us recall the characters of Heinrich von Kleist.

In the drama it is precisely the individual pathological case that assumes a distinctive, general validity. While the life of the average citizen is for the most part just the story of himself and quite without interest for anyone else, Ibsen's patients, even if to an exaggerated degree, do carry within themselves something that exists in us all. Hence his symbols sometimes reveal sudden, ineffable spiritual depths, sending a momentary shudder of self-recognition through us, when what we thought that what we were watching was an allegory or a pathological case. Now and then a sentence seems to come crashing down through several storeys and ends up coming to rest in the depths of our soul.

For it is often the case that in Ibsen's symbols something is liberated that can only be expressed in symbols, for example in the symbolism of dreams: the spiritual contents of the subconscious. Ibsen brought to the surface layers of the soul that could never have been uttered in the visual language of the older techniques of representing psychology. If we take his symbols literally, then he is one of the founders of modern psychology. These insights, these continuous self-recognitions are what give Ibsen's symbols, and the work of Ibsen generally, one of their most important values.

But what we have said so far does not exhaust our apologia for the symbols. These symbols are the most powerful elements of Ibsen's wondrous, wintry, pure, snow-covered landscape that is nevertheless illumined by a homely inner glow, whose sublime beauty encompasses everything connoted by that geographical symbol, Scandinavia, or more broadly the North. Vibrant in Ibsen's symbolism is an entire subcontinent, the spirit of an entire people, a great people. Inscrutability, a brooding, gloomy, incoherent yearning, a hopeless masculine melancholy, a Romanticism free of pathos: he is the new, great voice of the North, the new, starch-collared Ossian.

Embodied in a substantial proportion of Ibsen's later symbols are not just human thoughts and feelings, forces suggestive of the ultimate determinants of fate: Rosmer's death-horses, the tolling of Solness's bell at the top of the bell-tower, the Rat-Woman symbolizing the inexplicable attraction of danger in *Little Eyolf,* and Ellida's sea: these are quasi-mythic elements, embodiments of the great Forces of Nature like the Greek gods or, better, like their closer neighbours, the people of Odin, the giant people that howl in the wind. Peer Gynt grew wholly out of the northern saga and cannot be understood by those unable to enjoy him as a folktale like Petőfi's *János Vitéz,* for through his symbols pointing into the distance Ibsen in his old age returned to the folktale.

Therefore, the contents of the symbols can wear out, their significance from the point of view of dramatic technique can be lost, but from the lyrical angle the very fact of the creation of the symbol keeps it eternally fresh: thus is Ibsen's world, as it demolishes the walls of the bourgeois dining room, transformed into something enigmatic, infinite, permeated by the melodies of the infinite, a story-like something, superhuman. The Hungarian critic Frigyes Riedl said that a good poem is like a seashell: if you hold it to your ear you can hear the sound of the ocean. Some of Ibsen's plays are good poems of this kind: behind the symbols can be heard the ocean's distant roar.

Hence it is perhaps no exaggeration to suggest that Ibsen will endure for posterity not as a dramatist but as a dramatic poet. The social critical allegories to which he owed his renown, *The Wild Duck, The Doll's House, Ghosts,* and so forth, will sooner or later lose their power as their tenor becomes obsolete. The plays that will remain eternally young will be those in which we hear the voice of the lyrical Ibsen, his early plays, set in the storylands of the North, *The Vikings of Helgeland, The Pretenders,* and *Peer Gynt,* but especially the dramas of his old age, which are thinly disguised confessionals, uncontrollably inundating the lyric of the older Ibsen: *Rosmersholm, The Lady from the Sea, The Master Builder, Little Eyolf, John Gabriel Borkmann,* and *When We Dead Awaken.*

2.

Ibsen's lyricism. We all know and yet it remains true that the 'Ibsen atmosphere' is enigmatic, misty, and suggestive of faraway things. Although he was indeed one of the founders of dramatic realism, and although his vision of reality bordered on the ruthlessness of the neurologist, we might none the less say that his musical keynote was the escape from reality, the Romantic *sich fliehen.* The lyrical Ibsen is a Romantic soul. In dramatic form it was he who first most fully articulated the Romantics' basic temper, the Romantic gloom, the Romantic yearning to escape. Like all Romantics he too recoiled from his environment, the everyday, his reality;

he fled from it in his life, through his voluntary exile in his years spent in Rome and Munich; and he fled from it in his poetry.

Like all the Romantics, he was inspired above all by Yearning. Ossianic, northern melancholy, eternal, disquieting, half-admitted yearning colours the 'Ibsen mood'. This poet, cold in nature, buttoned up to the chin and armed to the teeth with thoughts, knew only one feeling: yearning, but this one feeling he was able to articulate in the world tearfully and with unparalleled intensity.

In the course of the Romantic century Romantic yearning underwent many shifts in form. The Romantic yearning at the beginning of the century still had in its sights the Blue Flower, the transcendent Unknown, the mystical reality lowering beyond and above life. For these writers material existence was incidental and that is why they could find a resolution in the Catholic afterlife. Ibsen is the child of a materialist and faithless age and belongs to the generation from which sprang the new Vitalism, the respect for life on earth based on metaphysics, heralding Nietzsche and Bergson. The neo-Romantic yearning does not desire to transcend the 'blazing borders of the world', but being the yearning of a poet, cannot be directed merely at things that are worldly and determinate. Ibsen (and Ibsen-age man) thirsts for life itself, all of life, the fullness of life, in which man can fully realize himself, transform all his abilities into deeds, gratifying every passion, burning up every moment in the ultimate flame of his being, and being totally engulfed by feeling, 'to the fingertips', as the German Romantics put it.

This kind of existence, however, existed for Ibsen always only as a yearning; it was never realized in his industrious and simple working life. Nor is it realized by his heroes; they too only yearn for it. To be more precise, Ibsen's lyricism is a *yearning for a life afar off.* Life with a capital letter filters into his poetry enigmatically and with painful consequences, as an invalid might hear from behind the closed and curtained windows of a room the pulsating life of the street.

An inkling of this yearning for a life afar can already be detected in the dramas of the young Ibsen: the fantasies of Peer Gynt, that make him such a dissembler, lazy and selfish, with which he rocks to death his fantasist of a mother, have as their goal Life with a capital letter, but the latter is possible only in dreams and Peer Gynt botches his life with a small letter because of this, without which it could have been so pleasant. Julian the Apostate (in *Emperor and Galilean*) wants to construct the Third Kingdom, the country of the Sun God, which would be the realm of Life with a capital letter, by uniting elements of Antiquity and Christianity; but his desire is broken on the wheel of necessity.

This motif is latent throughout the didactic dramas of Ibsen's middle period. It is perhaps at its most powerful in *Ghosts*, but there it is a sad caricature, taking the form of Oswald, with his seriously undermined constitution and his hopeless longing for the sun. In *Rosmersholm*, when Rosmer speaks of the country of noblemen, it is something like this that he has in mind, but is as yet unable to see clearly.

After *Rosmersholm* begins Ibsen's final turn towards the lyrical, with *The Lady from the Sea*. He was quite old by this time. He had achieved everything that a writer could: fame, riches, the triumph of his ideas to a certain degree, and what is even more important, the full realization of his artistic ego in his work; he had already created what he had to create. And yet he felt, as he did not disguise in his letters, that there was something he had failed to do, perhaps the most important thing: Life with a capital letter had passed him by and was now beyond recall. This is what all the plays of his old age are about.

Initially he dares speak only indirectly, in the guise of women's souls, for the eternal unquenched longing tends to be a female attribute. He creates, modelling her on himself, Ellida, the Lady from the Sea, who is tormented by a perpetual yearning for the Sea. The sea means many things: the sea itself, the sea of the soul, and passion, the other constantly raging and restless thing: life. Ellida is still able to resign herself, but the other woman, Hedda Gabler, cannot. She tries to realize on earth, in little Norway, Life with a capital letter; but her cowardice thwarts everything she tries to do, she is smothered by petty, unpleasant, pettifogging behaviour, and she flees into the only possible Act, suicide.

This was followed by the first open confession, his first true reckoning with himself, *The Master Builder*. All Solness has done throughout his life is build: churches for God, homes for others, but nothing for himself, and now he has been overtaken by old age. When youth finally knocks on his door it is too late: life has passed him by and his dizzy head cannot bear the heights.

The hero of *Little Eyolf*, Allmers, also realizes that he has sold himself for the sake of his work and allows the opportunity that Life with a capital letter has given him, in the form of little Eyolf, to flee in two alternative ways.

The eponymous hero of *John Gabriel Borkmann* is not creative like his siblings, the other characters of Ibsen's late works. He has been cut off from reality by the same things as most people in our age (and perhaps for this reason this is the easiest of his late plays to stage): the abstractions of Money and Power. None the less he too is Ibsen, in disguise.

Ibsen's epilogue, *When We Dead Awaken*, is a wholly candid, lyrical confession. Rubek-Ibsen, immediately before his death, re-lives in the ecstatic illumination of his approaching decline, how he has ruined his life, how he might have lived and yet never did. It is said that Ibsen laboured on this work with a feverish impatience, and in fact he died shortly before its completion. Perhaps he intended this as a prophetic last will and testament: to demonstrate to generations to come that his life was an object lesson in how not to live, that they should learn from it and not neglect their responsibility to life.

The life that Ibsen and the heroes speaking from his soul all long for is always afar, somewhere else: water creatures cast ashore look thus at the play of waves on the open sea. Some internal inhibition always prevents them from realizing themselves, from fulfilling their ever-distant, ever-restless desires. 'Every *sund* [sound, or channel leading to the sea] is closed to them,' to use Ibsen's favourite metaphor, to which he constantly harks back in his letters. But why, one wonders, could they never reach the sea?

Ibsen was much too intellectual a poet to content himself with simply asserting that inhibition was a fact of the soul without seeking some explanation for it. His explanations, dressed in allegorical form, can be summed up in two trains of thought.

Generally he set up his thesis in such a way that the creative artist has to choose between art and love; and if, following his inner laws, he chooses art, then he must forever lose love, the woman, intense, flowing, true life. This thought is a leitmotif throughout the nineteenth century, perhaps with its source, like everything else, in Goethe: Goethe's idyll of Sesenheim, the first time he sacrificed love implacably to his artistic ambitions, was the source of the Gretchen tragedy. It reaches its human and artistic apogee with Flaubert and the principle of *impassibilité* on the one hand, and on the other with Ibsen's most immediate precursor, Hebbel, who like a force of nature sacrificed every woman to his artistic selfishness, and by a curious paradox it was the latter who created in Rhodope and Mariamne the forerunners of *The Doll's House*'s Nora, who would rather be doomed than be a tool in a man's hands. This was not a problem that Ibsen succeeded in resolving: Gerhard Hauptmann, probably under Ibsen's influence, wrote *Gabriel Schilling*, whose anti-Rubek hero is ruined because he chooses love above art. Hauptmann's resolution of the problem is today perhaps closer to us; all the more so because the reality of lived life is much tenser in this, Hauptmann's best work, than in the aged Ibsen's, these being very much works trembling on mountain peaks whipped by the wind of glaciers and of mortality.

But this problem, like most of Ibsen's problems, is one that we can no longer feel to be a real one. This ability to choose freely between art and love is in fact a posteriori, something that in reality never existed. If Ibsen had chosen love, he would in the best case have been a happy man. And that is truly too little.

The inspiration of Ibsen's other train of thought begins with the character of Julian the Apostate: through the word 'conscience' Christian morality paralysed pagan Greek joy in life. A life lived untrammelled and to the full runs into external barriers in Christian society and internal ones in the Christian soul. Transgressing the external barriers would lead to anarchy, while crossing the internal ones would give rise to the kind of guilt feelings that would *ab ovo* spoil the taste of every delight. This is why Hedda Gabler is cowardly and why Solness is dizzy, unavailingly longing for the robust conscientiousness of his Viking ancestors.

Ibsen grew up in a pietistic environment and despite all his unbelief he carried his pietist conscience all his life 'like a corpse on his back', as he put it. We are none the less of the view that this was not the root cause of his inner inhibitions, and even if by some miracle he had been able to shake the corpse off his back he would not have lived a full life, for he was held back by emotional inhibitions even when his conscience did not raise warning objections — for example, in his married life, which is echoed in the glumly bleak, almost incomprehensibly paralysed family life of Solness, Allmers, and Borkmann.

The great barrier was that distinctive spiritual capacity which the European soul had promulgated in the course of centuries of Protestantism and pietism: a hypertrophied self-consciousness. Ibsen is the representative of the type of man who exercises a decisive influence on the intellectual history of our times. In particular, the type who pays most attention to his own soul and in the vast world of creation regards primarily his own soul as most worthy of contemplation. This type came into being thanks to a long period of religious culture but in the course of time became detached from its religious roots. Self-observation, which was originally directed at the duality, hidden within us, of good and evil, became something pursued for its own sake, reaching beyond good and evil. And the further it became detached from religion, the further it moved away from the reality of life, because self-observation bleaches out the colour of the spiritual content that is being observed: if I observe myself when I am being angry, I cannot be truly angry, if I observe myself when I am loving, I cannot be truly in love — and in the end self-observation becomes the sole, dark, cold passion of the soul. And this was to be Ibsen's fate, too.

It was not his fault. He was a martyr to himself; a martyr to an unfortunate age, the age of individualism, which found no higher idol to worship than the self. No one depicted more tragically the self-abandonment of his age, its abandonment of and by God; the great Aphelion, the painfully insuperable distance that separated the age from life and from all that is imperishable in perishable life. In the character of Jarl Skule he passed the most comprehensive judgement on himself: 'He was God's stepson on earth'.

Notes to Chapter 7

1. [First published in *Napkelet*, 7 (1 April 1928).]
2. ['For my love I'll sacrifice | My life, | For freedom I'll sacrifice | My love', Gyula Illyés, *Petőfi*, trans. by G. F. Cushing (Budapest: Corvina, 1973), p. 270.]

CHAPTER 8

Dulcinea (Cervantes) (1936)[1]

'Dulcinea del Toboso is the most beauteous lady and I am the most unfortunate knight in all of Spain.' This is the entirety of a passage that recently came to my attention, from the vast amount of lyrical, epic, and chiefly pseudo-philosophical debris of my diary.

This is a diary I kept when I was at university. When writing it I was convinced it would be of enormous value to me later, because it would bring back the sweet (and less sweet) joys and sorrows of my youth, but this was mistaken, like so much else I believed and professed at that time. I took the diary out again not long ago, and apart from one quotation it left me completely cold. Any good novel would draw me in far more. As raw material for my writing now it is no more useful to me than the diary of a stranger. We seem, over time, to lose our feeling for our own past.

This quotation stands quite without context in the diary's contents. Both before and after it can be read the incipient symptoms of a great love, a truly great love, whose genuineness at the time I have no reason to doubt. It is precisely for that reason that I am still astonished today by the sort of prophetic presentiment, that sudden, inexplicable premature emergence of my future self from the womb of time, which made me write out the quotation at a time when I could have had no inkling of the Don Quixotic nature of my love-besotted self.

Nor did I have any notion of this until I read Cervantes's wonderful work all the way through and discovered not only something that until then I had only suspected on the basis of what György Lukács and other specialist heavyweights had said, namely who really was Don Quixote, that beloved ancestor of us all, but also the secret that until then no one had yet let me into: who was, and still is, Dulcinea del Toboso.

I must first ask you, dear reader, to erase from your memory for the next few minutes your childhood recollections of Don Quixote, because they are mis-leading. Those renowned adventures — the tilting at windmills, which has become part of the language, the heroic dispersal of the flock of sheep, the flight on the wooden horse that never moves, the puppet theatre smashed to smithereens — these occupy a surprisingly, indeed vanishingly small place in the whole work. Because Don Quixote is no mad fantasist and Sancho Panza is no gluttonous and cowardly peasant. This was the misconception that Cervantes himself protested against most vehemently when, following the publication of his work, some crass scribbler, misunderstanding Cervantes's intentions, concocted a sequel depicting Don Quixote as a madman and Sancho Panza as a common peasant.

It cannot even been be maintained — although a number of quotations may be adduced in support — that Don Quixote is not entirely mad but a victim of some obsession. (Most recently two French doctors subjected Don Quixote to a psycho-pathological examination and stated their conclusions in terms of the meaningless banalities that are usually the outcome when medical psychologists encroach upon literary psychology. They established that Don Quixote was paranoid and a megalomaniac — which is like claiming that he had two legs but only one head.)

Don Quixote is such a problematic individual that even about his obsession, his Quixoticness, we must have our doubts. He is by no means the kind of madman who would embrace a blazing hot stove. This can be seen from the splendid scene where the knight believed to be mad makes advance preparations to start raving. He wants to rave, because his knightly models also from time to time went raving mad in their disconsolate love. Sancho tries to discourage him by saying that Dulcinea has given him no reason to rave (although, equally, no reason not to). To this the knight replies that he differs from the other knights precisely because they undertook their raving madness on their beloved's account only when they had reason, whereas his raving is entirely spontaneous and for no reason at all. It is, in any event, reasonable to go raving mad, he says, because if Sancho returns from Dulcinea with good news, he will come to his senses and rejoice, and if he returns with bad news, then he will remain mad and be simply unable to understand anything and thus spare himself sorrow. After this he muses on whether he should indeed formally go raving mad, like Orlando of old, or merely weep, like Amadis of Gaul. In the end he decides that to go raving mad is the more effective course, but he does not carry his raving madness to excess and just raves in a careful and dignified manner, turning a cartwheel or two, after which he orders Sancho to promulgate the matter, suitably embellished, in the appropriate forums.

Don Quixote is a madman who at the same time stands above and outside his mania. He does not take himself entirely seriously and does not place full credence in himself. On the other hand, neither is it possible to say that he is playing the fool and fooling the world. His truth is true in a way that is other than normal. Having been lowered into the cave of Montesinos, on his return he recounts to Sancho a wondrous vision, after which to the very last he ponders how much of what he has said was true and how much not. He is so troubled by this question that he even seeks the view of Merlin, the magician of King Arthur's court, about it.

Not only does Cervantes not regard Don Quixote as mad; he is prepared on occasion to treat him as one of the elite, one of humankind's elect and unfortunate luminaries. Don Quixote not only apes the chivalrous ideal but is actually possessed of truly chivalric virtues himself: he is brave to the point of recklessness, profoundly chivalrous towards the fair sex, always ready to fight on behalf of the oppressed, of a generous disposition, ready to make sacrifices, and charmingly courteous in both word and deed: King Arthur would surely be satisfied with him if they met. At the same time there already reside in him newer, more recent, more modern, and more humane aspirations than those of chivalry: those belonging to the world of the humanist revolutionary, the reformer, the nineteenth-century idealist. An example of this is his liberation of the prisoners and his willingness to accept punishment for this good deed in the same way as the serf-liberating landowners of Kemény and Tolstoy.

György Lukács and more recently Thomas Mann have seen him as a doctrinaire idealist bankrupt of ideas in practical terms. His inner world is far more circumscribed than the outside world, and on that, according to Lukács, he founders. In the words of Thomas Mann: 'Everything that Don Quixote says is good and reasonable, but everything he does is nonsensical, foolhardy and silly, and one almost gets the impression that he wants to pose as the natural and inevitable antithesis of the poet of the higher moral life'.[2]

They are doubtless right. But there is something they do not articulate, leaving the feeling of close kinship I have for Don Quixote unexplained. For I am neither doctrinaire nor an idealist and my words and actions are generally in inverse proportion to those of Don Quixote, that is to say, my words are less carefully considered and rational than my actions.

The characteristics of the Don Quixote with whom I feel this kinship emerge far more clearly if I try to approach the novel from the literary historical perspective. Cervantes's novel is the most important turning point in the history of the novel. Before it, the novel had been a treasure house of wonderful fictions, a veritable fish tank of magical knights errant and enchanted princesses. These are the Amadis-novels and it is against these that Cervantes takes up arms. But his campaign takes the form of 'I've caught a Turk but now he won't let me go'.[3] The fairytale world of the Amadis-novels finds its way into *Don Quixote*, as every single adventure of the knight of La Mancha is a parody of some adventure in one of those, the difference being that in the latter the enchanted world behaves as if it were objective reality, whereas in Cervantes the reality is subjective. It is Don Quixote's *idée fixe*. This is the first appearance of psychology in novel-writing. Cervantes depicts not only things that occur in the outside world, but also those that occur inside in the hero's soul.

This much is self-evident and well known. What is more important for the moment is that Cervantes's novel is the first work of literature in which two parallel worlds are presented. Hitherto literature had been enacted in only one world: historical works in the world of reality, novels only in that of wonders. The writer of history took reality seriously, the writer of novels took the wonders seriously. Cervantes was the first to take both seriously or rather, he took neither seriously — the world he took seriously was that third one, symbolized, as we shall see, by Dulcinea del Toboso.

In his novel are two conflicting realities: one reality is that of Don Quixote and the other is, shall we say, that of Sancho Panza. Usually it is the latter that gets called reality. But viewed through Don Quixote's eyes, the other is the true one.

Panza's reality, to which the author, too, tends to subscribe, offers some supporting evidence to prove itself the more real. It is crude, clodhopping evidence. Don Quixote collides headlong with Panza's reality, which he ignores, and thus comes to grief. The evidence is primarily the recurrent and regular pastings endured by the Knight of Mournful Mien and his sidekick: the Panza reality's symbolic and at the same time Panza-like, petty-minded, grotesque revenge.

However, Quixote's world also proffers Evidence with a capital E to prove that, even in defeat, it is the more real. This evidence is of a refined and intellectual kind: the concept of enchantment. If Sancho Panza sees Mambrino's helmet as a barber's basin, if the giants they attack behave like a windmill, if the defeated army of pagans is alleged to be a herd of sheep and compensation must be paid, then Don Quixote is always clear that a wicked wizard has a hand in it so as to ruin his reputation. Panza's reality seen from the point of view of Don Quixote is an evil phantasmagoria conjured forth by magicians.

The discovery of the 'two worlds' is much more than a chapter in the history of the novel. It is the birth of a new type of human being, the 'modern', or 'Romantic', or 'Baroque', or call it what you will. Soon the painters of the Baroque will also light upon those two worlds and from the two opt for Panza's world, that of face values. Artists become ever more conscious of the inner divide. Agrippa D'Aubigné's dialogues (1617) take place between the two gentlemen Einay (*einai* — being/reality) and Faeneste (*phainestai* — appearance), and further links in the chain continue to the Romantics, the Peter Schlemihl who sells his own shadow, and on to E. T. A. Hoffmann's 'Doppelgänger', which then becomes a model for Dostoevsky. The modern novel of Proust, Joyce, and Musil is nothing but a vast Doppelgänger-tale about the hopeless chasm between the inner and outer man.

Don Quixote is only mad to the extent that any innovator is mad. He is as mad as Florence Nightingale must have been in the Crimean War when she arrived with her nurses to tend to the wounded, whereupon, offended, all the doctors, with Panzaic reality, went stalking out of the hospital with mocking laughter. Were Don Quixote to visit us today, every literary coterie would welcome him with open arms.

But only in literary circles would he enjoy success. I am sure that in ministries or textile factories he would be regarded much as he was then. For Don Quixote was every inch a literary man.

For the whole enormous splitting apart, the working loose of the Quixote world and its breaking off from the more ancient Panza-reality has been achieved through belles-lettres. At that time belles-lettres consisted of the Amadis-novel of which Don Quixote was so fond. And actually Cervantes, too, for when the priest performs his auto-da-fé over the books, he spares most of them; and at the beginning of the second volume Cervantes sings the novel's praises in a manner scarcely paralleled in world literature. The world of Quixote, which György Lukács abstractly calls the world of abstract ideas is in fact the world of books. Don Quixote is a man of the book.

Cervantes's diabolical irony plays a grotesque and ambiguous game with Don Quixote's man-of-the-book nature. Don Quixote is not just a man *of* the book but at the same time a man *in* a book. A man who lives in a novel and simultaneously knows that he is the hero of a novel. The greatest adventures in the second volume presuppose that the characters who appear in it have read the first volume and also, perhaps, its fraudulent continuation by another hand. The duke's warm welcome is for the popular hero of the novel. The duke is the virtuoso sport of the novel's mirror-world — he organizes a Quixotic world around Don Quixote, who is ultimately reassured that he is in the right as a result. As a matter of fact even Panza is converted to Don Quixote's faith, when he is indeed appointed the governor of an island as Don Quixote had promised. Even his sad demise the Don owes to the fact that he is a character in a novel. His life must come to an end lest some incompetent hand again writes a poor sequel.

Et nunc venio ad fortissimam.

Dulcinea is distinguished from nearly all the heroines in the world's novels by a most interesting property: she is only discussed and never makes a personal appearance on the scene. Or rather, perhaps she does so just once, but this is uncertain, a topic to which we shall return. I certainly cannot recall any other novel with such an elusive heroine; only Maurice Baring's *Daphne Adeane* or Clemence Dane's *Legend* may be candidates. But both of those English novels saw the light of day after the revitalization of the novel by Gide and Joyce and in them the non-appearance of the heroine is an intentional and very engaging literary trick. The heroines' characters are (re)constructed, before the reader's very eyes, from the traces they left behind in the awareness of their loved ones, for about human beings themselves we can know nothing and that is the point. 'Arctic cold, secrecy, alienation'.[4] We can know of them only as much as is reflected in ourselves: the speck of dust that has dropped from their ego into our own consciousness and around which in time has grown a pearl, the treasure of the oceans, a legend.

That Cervantes too was somehow thinking along these lines we know from one of the outstanding sections of the novel. The kindly duchess asks Don Quixote whether the beauteous Dulcinea truly exists or is just a phantom, a poetic fancy. We, the readers, know that Dulcinea is truly present in this world, in the objective Panza-world, too. For she had been admired by Don Quixote — sometime long ago, since love always has its origins a long time ago in the past — before he became possessed by his mania for chivalry. And Cervantes's fictional source, Cide Hamete Benengeli, wrote of her that she was an excellent sausage-maker, there was no one far and wide who could salt pork so well as the person that Don Quixote called Dulcinea. And yet with the lunatic wisdom of his being Don Quixote replies to the duchess with the words: 'God knows whether there be any Dulcinea or not in the world, or whether she is imaginary or not imaginary; these are things the proof of which must not be pushed to extreme lengths'.[5]

Again we find ourselves confronting the same duality or cleavage as in the legerdemain of the madness scene: Don Quixote is on the one hand (the Panza side) crazy, a fantast, who sees Fair Helen in a peasant girl; on the other hand he is far more sane than the folk of the Panza–reality, indeed ferociously sane. He knows with the cool clear-sightedness of genius that Dulcinea, accepted by those of the Panza-reality as an existing being, in reality does not exist, or at least not simply and one-sidedly: she is not the Dulcinea that the duchess is inquiring after.

Dulcinea both exists and does not exist. Somewhere in Toboso is a peasant girl who stuffs sausages, and there is in Don Quixote's psyche a Dulcinea-complex. But the real Dulcinea is virtually independent of both and does not exist in fact but rather possesses, in the sense that Ákos Pauler used the word, validity. And it is towards this curious Dulcinea, enthroned on the cusp of two worlds, alien in both,

inaccessible in both to those passing through, that Don Quixote's longing soars —
and such is the Dulcinea of every man possessed of a soul.

Now, anyone who thinks that Don Quixote 'idealized' the person of the 'real'
Dulcinea and that this idealized Dulcinea 'exists in Don Quixote's imagination',
is fearfully misguided; but such a misunderstanding is natural — and fatal. This
is how the historians of religion misunderstood the gods of old. This is how the
historians of art misunderstood the age of Raphael. This is how the historians of
literature misunderstood the 'ideal forms' of the poetry of Goethe and Vörösmarty.
The philistine is unable to comprehend that genius — whether creating a god or a
work of art — does not idealize, because to idealize means to consciously express
something other than what I see, to deliberately tamper with reality. And he
cannot trust his imagination, because the imagination asserts untruths in much the
same way as idealization. Idealization and the aesthetics of the imagination are the
progeny of a secondary Romanticism, the mid-century and the age of philistinism.
Both are based on the notion of 'the beautiful lie' — and genius never lies.

An example will make everything clear. Don Quixote entrusts Sancho Panza
with finding Dulcinea and bringing a message from her. Panza is too lazy to go
to Toboso and being a philistine leaves matters to his imagination and returns to
Don Quixote with a message that is a lie. Later they go together to Toboso. Panza
dares not admit that he has never been to these parts and never seen Dulcinea, and
so devises a stratagem. When three peasant girls come their way in the meadow,
he exclaims: here comes Dulcinea in all her finery, accompanied by two of her
ladies-in-waiting. Don Quixote demurs, saying all he can see is three peasant girls.
Panza now brilliantly turns the Quixote evidence against him, declaring that, in
that case, someone has obviously cast a spell over his master, some powerful enemy
of his has doomed him to see Dulcinea as an ordinary peasant girl, just as Panza
saw Mambrino's helmet as an ordinary barber's basin. Don Quixote, hoist by his
own petard, is compelled to face the facts. He asserts peevishly that he seems to
be seeing Dulcinea hopping onto her mule, legs akimbo, with the sprightliness of
a peasant girl, just after his olfactory delusion that Dulcinea smelled of garlic. And
later, when he has his remarkable vision in the cave of Montesinos, Dulcinea del
Toboso appears to him, not, however, as the young mistress of his dreams but as a
peasant girl who bewails her wretched bewitched lot and immediately requests a
sum of money to buy herself a new skirt.

Now, if Don Quixote had wished to 'idealize' the figure of Dulcinea, he would
have had no better opportunity to do so than in this half-real, half-invented vision:
here he could have made up for all his failures and, in knight-errantly obeisance,
knelt at the feet of the idol, his ideal. But this is not what happened. Dulcinea,
independently of both the Panza-reality and Don Quixote's wishful thinking,
saw fit to clothe herself in and appear under the guise wished upon her by Sancho
Panza's lies. The poetic imagination of the author, by the way, leaves us unsure
whether one of the three peasant girls was not in fact Dulcinea. And by doing so
he offers us his final piece of wisdom: it does not matter. The Dulcinea beloved of
Don Quixote is to be identified neither with the peasant girl of Toboso nor with
the knight errant's daydream. She is Love itself. A speck of dust has fallen into Don

Quixote's heart and a pearl has grown around it. He is no more able to interrupt or influence its formation than the direction of a dream or a legend.

Love — our love — focuses not on the actual woman *secundum Panzam*, still less on its 'heavenly reflection', but on the unfathomable daemonic legend, the transcendent body of woman, arching rainbow-like between two worlds.

Notes to Chapter 8

1. [First published in *Sziget*, 2 (April 1936).]
2. 'Alles was Don Quijote sagt, ist gut und vernünftig, aber alles was er tut, unsinnig, tollkühn and albern, und fast hat man den Eindruck, als ob er Dichter das als eine natürliche und unvermeidliche Antinomie des höhern moralischen Lebens hinstellen wollte.' Thomas Mann, *Meerfahrt mit Don Quijote,* in his *Leiden und Größe der Meister* (Berlin, 1935).
3. [A Hungarian saying, approximately: 'hoist with one's own petard'.]
4. [From Endre Ady's famous poem, 'Sem utódja, sem boldog őse' [Neither Descendant nor Joyful Ancestor].]
5. [Miguel de Cervantes, *The Ingenious Gentleman Don Quixote of La Mancha*, trans. by John Ormsby, 4 vols (London: Smith Elder & Co., 1885), III, p. 356.]

CHAPTER 9

G. K. Chesterton (1929)[1]

The recent death of Gilbert Keith Chesterton has robbed us of one of the most notable and interesting personalities of English literary life in recent decades. With his novels, journalism, short stories, and studies he unceasingly amused, enlightened, and disconcerted his public and, perhaps even more importantly, it is a distinctive, old-style and writerly persona and an exceptional human being who emerges from his writings. For all his attractive kindliness, informality, and indeed workaday plainness, he remained enigmatic enough to suggest considerable depth.

Let us picture to ourselves Chesterton in the last decade and a half of his career: an exceptionally overweight, bespectacled, yet jovial English gentleman perched on the podium (for Chesterton was an impassioned lecturer and orator), pouring forth an endless stream of jokes, startling turns of phrase, paradoxes, and preposterous similes, all the while drinking water like a fish, his face streaming with perspiration, and continually wiping the spectacles which he then replaces with a comical gesture. This is the Chesterton who stands before us, a curious cross between great scholar and sophisticated clown. The wise and witty court jesters of the great kings of yore must have been such. And at the same time this man was the bearer and champion of mystical truths, a faithful propagator of a faith: a clown, but *God's clown*, as were once the most zealous followers of St Francis.

Thus even in his personal behaviour was apparent the form of expression he preferred and of which he was one of the outstanding practitioners: the paradox. In recent English literature paradox has played an especially important role. Oscar Wilde, in the closing years of the nineteenth century, brought into fashion wit expressed by means of a seeming contradiction. Wilde poured forth paradoxes purely as wit for wit's sake — *l'art pour l'art* — and had no wish to make them proclaim the truth of any construct, as he believed in none, only in the principle of art for art's sake. The next stage in the history of the English paradox comes with George Bernard Shaw, for whom the paradox was no longer a goal in itself but a means by which to fight for his ideas. Shaw was born in the same year as Wilde but arrived on the scene and achieved fame as a writer somewhat later. At the outset of his literary career he fought his major crusade against exactly the kind of wit that Wilde represented: the decadents, the aesthetes, and in general the flaccid, weak-willed, and laboured hopelessness of the *fin de siècle*, and in that battle he turned against his opponents their own ammunition, the paradox.

And so Shaw assassinated Wilde, the first master of the paradox, with his own weapon. Something similar happened to him in turn, when the third great master of the paradox, Chesterton, came on the scene. The parallel is imperfect in that not only did Shaw outlive Chesterton, eighteen years his junior, but his *oeuvre*, too, will probably outlive Chesterton's, as it is more challenging and also of greater worth. Nor did Chesterton's campaign seek to massacre Shaw as Shaw did in the case of the decadents. He always had the greatest respect for him, wrote a whole book about him and was always referring to him: no one exerted a greater influence on him than Shaw. But there is no doubt that just as Shaw's paradoxes were more daring than Wilde's, Chesterton's far surpassed Shaw's in audacity and surprise effect, and in this sense we may say that he went one better and, as it were, vanquished Shaw with his own weapon. And this triumph is itself all the more paradoxical because, whereas Shaw's paradoxes were startling, Chesterton surprised the world precisely by invariably launching the light cavalry of his paradoxes in defence of the most unsurprising, most widely accepted, and traditional truths.

Shaw, as we know, in his younger days advocated progress in every way. He has since then revised his convictions in many respects. But at that time he was still on the side of the new: in the confrontation between religion and science, he stood for science, in politics he was on the left, if there was discussion of the guiding principles of existence he always sided with the rational against the emotional. No one did more to defeat that greatest of nineteenth-century intellectual legacies, sentimentalism. In art and life-style, too, he was always an adherent of everything new. He enthused equally about Ibsen, Wagner, and vegetarianism. He accepted nothing traditional without — and most often not even after — questioning it. In everything he took a stand against tradition and sterile convention. Chesterton encapsulated Shaw's 'modernity' in a bon mot: 'if Shaw had found in early life that he was contradicted by *Bradshaw's Railway Guide* or even by the *Encyclopaedia Britannica*, he would have felt at least that he might be wrong. But if he had found himself contradicted by his father and mother, he would have thought it all the more probable that he was right'.

Chesterton, by contrast, from the outset took up arms against the proponents of progress. It was not, of course, progress itself that incensed him but his contemporaries, who idolized and fetishized progress: those intent on progress at all costs, not towards something better, but simply for its own sake, in other words because they simply made a fetish of it. 'Out of the primal forests,' he wrote, 'through all the real progress of history, man had picked his way obeying his human instinct, or (in the excellent phrase) following his nose. But now he was trying, by violent athletic exertions, to get in front of his nose.'

He did not do battle against dead conventions but took their part. Besides, dead conventions did not exist. 'Conventions may be cruel,' he wrote in his essay *The Philosopher*, 'they may be unsuitable, or they may even be grossly superstitious or obscene; but there is one thing they never are. Conventions are never dead. They are always full of accumulated emotions, the piled-up and passionate experiences of many generations.'

Chesterton claims to be a degree more sober than even Shaw, renowned for his sobriety. His own simile likens himself to a rake who stays up later and later, ending up so depraved that it is nine in the evening before he is in bed. Chesterton considered sound good sense, too, to be a fabrication, even if accepted in good faith, an outdated superstition of the eighteenth-century Enlightenment. Therefore, in the battle between rationality and emotion he sides with emotion, and in that between sound good sense and Romanticism, with Romanticism, because the latter shows more sound good sense.

Chesterton became as passionate and militant a devotee of tradition as Shaw its iconoclast. With his extravagant paradoxes his aim was to make the ideals of Christianity, the national English way of thinking, of the beleaguered social order alleged to be outdated, valuable once more in the eyes of people inclined rather to call themselves modern. In those of his writings concerned with social issues he advocated a distinctive middle way, a middle way ordained by tradition and history. He was not attracted by the newfangled socialism, but was even more repelled by the equally newfangled large-scale plutocracy, declaring it essential to return to the economic order of those centuries when the rich were not overwhelmingly rich and the poor were not overwhelmingly poor and to seek the golden mean in everything: medium-sized estates instead of latifundia and dwarf land-holdings, moderate-sized workshops and old-style tradesmen rather than huge emporia and factories. 'We are no longer a nation of shopkeepers,' he quipped in his book on Blake, 'but merely a nation of shop-owners.'

A fundamental experience, as with so many English writers and artists, was nostalgia for the Middle Ages. In one of his later novels, *The Return of Don Quixote*, the protagonist sets off to buy certain paints used in his childhood. But these artisan paints are not available anywhere and it had been a long time since the large stores stocked them. Don Quixote *redivivus*, after circuitous wanderings, comes upon an elderly paint-shop-owner in a small seaside town who still manufactures the old colours. He arrives just in time to save him from being committed to a lunatic asylum. Chesterton, too, was in love with those ancient colours and tormented by nostalgic longing for the blue in which the Virgin Mary was celebrated and the crimson of the ducal tournaments.

Chesterton often employed audacious paradoxes to demonstrate that Romantic nostalgia is indeed the loftiest form of sound good sense.

In his book about America, for example, he argues that the famous bright lights of the advertisements on New York's Broadway are not, as the aesthetes assert, ugly but useful, but, on the contrary, beautiful but useless. They are beautiful because they transform New York into a fairy-tale castle that disappears at dawn, but useless, or will become so, as soon as people's sound good sense ends their belief that one brand of chewing gum is superior because its manufacturer makes this claim in bright lights.

Apart from nostalgia for the Middle Ages, Chesterton's other fundamental experience was a yearning for order. No one abhorred more the intellectual turmoil of our time, the anarchy at the heart of us. By 'order' is not, of course, meant philistine methodicalness and uniformity, which he abhorred most of all, but rather the world order which in the High Middle Ages allocated to each human being and value a precise place in society and even geography. Dante, for example, knew the exact location, circle, status, and definition of every vice and virtue.

Chesterton's respect for tradition and Romanticism inevitably led him to the place where the tradition of the eternally Romantic and, simultaneously, of order everlasting is preserved in the most pristine manner: the Catholic Church. Ideas akin to Catholicism can be found in his work from early on, but in 1922 he formally became a convert.

It is often said that in his Catholicism, too, there was a kind of search for paradox, and that perhaps he would not have felt it necessary to become a Catholic had England not happened to be a Protestant country. There was indeed about him something of the *jongleur de Dieu*, as he called St Francis in his splendid study. He too liked to stand on his head sometimes, like St Francis when he came out of prison. If we stand on our heads, he says, though we may see things upside down, yet at the same time the colours are brighter and, as objects are jolted out of their usual context, we feel more acutely how everything is truly in God's hands. Nonetheless his faith was that of a steadfast human being, serious and profound, who has trodden the path of paradox and reached a point unattainable by the human mind.

Chesterton's devoutness, however, by no means entailed draconian principles or dour moral precepts. On the contrary: in his conversion a large part was played by the fact that Catholicism is the religion of Southern Europe, whose people are more alive to the beauty of existence, whereas Protestantism is that of the continent's bleaker North. From the outset Chesterton felt a particular aversion for the moral constraints of English Calvinism generally spoken of as 'puritanism'. A puritan is one whose conscience pricks him whenever he is enjoying himself. In England puritanical traditions are even today extremely strong, in evidence not only in strict Sabbatarianism but in the way they pervade every aspect of the English psyche, literature no less than social intercourse, to crippling effect. What Chesterton emphasizes in Catholicism is precisely that it sanctifies decent and moderate *joie de vivre* and releases us from puritanical inhibitions.

That is how something at first glance remote from Chesterton's conceptual world fits in. This is beer, which played a very important part both in his life and his socio-literary activities. He consumed vast quantities of beer and the question of beer also loomed large in his writing. It should be remembered that in England stiff taxation makes beer a very expensive commodity, and additionally the times when it may be dispensed are strictly and irksomely regulated. It is impossible to obtain beer or other alcoholic beverages in the morning and afternoon, or after 11 o'clock at night. Chesterton saw in these provisions the despicable excesses of the puritan spirit, that of those English folk who suffer pangs of conscience at every joy affecting themselves or their fellows. Whereas in his view beer is such a good friend and immense solace to poorer people that the state should use every means at its disposal to make it widely available. In Chesterton's view the English puritans drink in the wrong way: they consume far too much and are far too ashamed of themselves for doing so. It would be better if they drank somewhat less and felt a deal less ashamed about it.

The work of Chesterton that has appeared in book form comprises partly critical studies and partly tales of adventure and detective-style novels and short stories. Some of his literary output is devoted to great figures in English literature: he wrote books about Dickens and Browning, as well as the eighteenth-century mystic poet and engraver William Blake, who composed his vast heroic epics at the dictation of the angels as he reposed on the shores of eternity. Chesterton also wrote about his great model and sparring partner, Bernard Shaw, and was the author of a witty, concise history of England. In his Catholic phase he devoted glorious books to St Francis of Assisi and St Thomas Aquinas. There are also several collections of his shorter studies and essays on a wide variety of topics.

For the general public it is probably his short stories that have the greatest appeal, and a number of these, as well as a collection of his critical essays, have appeared in Hungarian translation. While there is no essential difference between Chesterton the writer of scholarly dissertations and Chesterton the author of narrative prose, he composed a very distinctive kind of short story for his purposes, and this was perhaps his most paradoxical achievement of all: for he treated the traditional adventure and detective story, the thriller, in a manner suitable for the promulgation of his world view and the expression of his artistic persona. The detective stories he devised were humorous, yet (or perhaps for that reason) deadly serious in content. His detective stories are undoubtedly the most interesting ever written — but not *as* detective stories, because as such they are perhaps excessively whimsical and droll. He constantly violated the strict rules of the genre: Conan Doyle would certainly not have been proud of him.

The hero of his detective story series is the genial Father Brown. Father Brown is an exceedingly kindly, simple, and devout English friar, who lacks worldly wisdom to the point of extreme vulnerability and willy-nilly gets mixed up in the most curious criminal cases and manages to solve mysteries that would defeat even the wiliest of Sherlock Holmeses with playful ease thanks to his erudition and innocence but, in the main, to his Catholic piety. The most astonishing thing about all this is that, somehow, the solution almost always does indeed follow from Catholic precepts. The culprits are mainly heretics in some way and it is their hereticism that provides Father Brown with his clues.

Chesterton had no great opinion of his crime-writer forebears and fellows and particularly loathed clever Sherlock Holmes, who always worked on the basis of facts. 'Facts,' he wrote, 'point in all directions, it seems to me, like the thousands of twigs on a tree. It's only the life of the tree that has unity and goes up — only the green blood that springs, like a fountain, at the stars.' In his view what matters in a good detective story is not facts but instinctive perception, the intuition that Father Brown brought to bear.

The high point in Chesterton's literary career is his Father Brown stories, particularly his first collection, *The Innocence of Father Brown*, another of his volumes available in Hungarian. But even before his Catholic period he wrote a number of memorable tales of adventure, of which the first was *The Club of Queer Trades*. This is in fact a story within a story: we meet in turn, in the context of their startling adventures, each of the individuals who might be members of that club. A retired major called Brown, who is very fond of pansies, passes a garden in which these flowers have been planted so as to form letters spelling out the message 'Death to Major Brown'. Stunned, he rushes into the villa behind the garden and finds there a young woman who must sit in the window looking out on the street every day until six in the evening. At six a terrifying voice intones: Major Brown, Major Brown, where is the jackal? Major Brown hurries after the owner of the voice with whom he does battle in a dark coal cellar. He is fortunate to escape with his life. In the end it turns out that there has been a mistake: there is a man whose 'trade' is to provide unexpected romantic adventures to those grown bored with the monotony of life in the metropolis. This adventure had been ordered by a different Brown and our major found himself involved in it in error. Another club member's trade is equipping tree-houses, while two others are paid 'hinderers', engaged to order so as to delay with preposterous stories persons about to leave for a visit until they have missed their lunch or dinner that it is in someone's interests not to attend. From all these tales there emerges clearly the basic Chestertonian experience: the yearning for stronger, more vivid colours, the soul's ancestral Romanticism.

One of his most atmospheric novels is *The Napoleon of Notting Hill*. This is set in the future, when the English people choose their ruler by drawing lots. Their choice happens to fall on a Romantic Chestertonian jester who begins his reign by granting its own charter of independence, coat-of-arms, and flag to each London borough, as enjoyed by medieval towns. At first people scoff, but soon the idea finds fanatical supporters, and the militant, bloodthirsty, and self-sacrificing patriots of the various quarters of the city begin to exterminate each other in gory battle.

More remarkable still is the novel *The Man Who Was Thursday*, another available in Hungarian translation, the story of the unmasking of an anarchist conspiracy. By the time all the anarchists have been exposed it transpires that they are all detectives who thought the others to be anarchists. They had all been dispatched on their pointless quest by the mysterious police chief seated in a dark room, Sunday: God, with whom that purposeless heroism, that unending, spiritual crusading, finds favour.

As these accounts suggest, a somewhat poetic atmosphere reigns in Chesterton's stories. Anyone reading these and his studies, where scenes and arguments of astonishing poetic beauty can crop up when they are least expected, feels this particularly acutely. For Chesterton was a great poet; indeed, he was primarily a poet, in the strictest sense of the word, moreover. His verse is concerned less with lyrical self-expression than the rhetorical promulgation of his ideas, yet there are lines in it of considerable significance. His poems may well prove to be the most enduring of all his work. It is in them that his Romantic imagination, offbeat humour, and ceaseless yearning for the more vibrant landscape of the past find their purest and freest expression. This is hardly surprising, considering that if we sum up what we have said about Chesterton so far — his sparring with George Bernard Shaw, his rejection of so-called modern man and his ideas, his longing for the vitality of the Middle Ages and the orderliness of Catholicism — we can encapsulate the whole man in a single word: poet.

His opposition was that of the poet to a humanity turned prosaic.

Note to Chapter 9

1. [First published in Antal Szerb, *Az angol irodalom kistükre* [A Brief Survey of English Literature] (Budapest: Magyar Szemle Társaság, 1929). An earlier, shorter version entitled 'An English Conservative Writer: Chesterton' was published in *Magyar Szemle*, 2 (February 1928).]

CHAPTER 10

Katherine Mansfield (1931)[I]

The literary *oeuvre* of Katherine Mansfield is not extensive: a few volumes of short stories and her posthumously published diary and correspondence.

Her short stories belong in that aesthetic category about which it is difficult to say anything other than that they are wonderful. If wonderful were not in itself a superlative one might perhaps say that they are very wonderful. Any critical assessment, description, or analysis would seem offensively intellectual in comparison with her stories' miraculous simplicity. Perhaps unseemly also, like discussing a beautiful woman in terms of her intellectual capacities.

'The high luxury of not having to explain,' she writes in her diary, tersely and for no particular reason. Her short stories have no explanation. They are phenomena, like other phenomena in this world, without a reason yet brimful of meaning, like a river at sunset.

Ten years ago we would have said that there is in these short stories a tragic *Lebensgefühl*. Since expressions like this have become trite, it is difficult to say what we find in Katherine Mansfield's short stories. A kind of genuine, exquisite melancholy, for which we no longer have a name. At one time people spoke of melancholic humour; a hundred years later, of a sensitive heart.

The history of women writers is inseparable from that of the women's movement. Women, like other oppressed varieties of human beings, cannot rid themselves of the awareness that they are women. A woman's writerly attitude develops in line with the view she adopts vis-à-vis the fact of her female gender.

The spokeswomen for the first generation who fought for the equal rights of women were committed, bewhiskered hermaphrodites, bravely and vociferously prepared to starve to death for their right to vote. They wore men's hats and demanded men's rights. Their ideal was to be as men are. The newer generation wants to remain women. They do not even aspire to be ugly. This is the psychology of every awakening of self-awareness. The first of those in the history of Hungarian literature who deliberately wrote in Hungarian, from Bessenyei to Kölcsey, wanted to write Hungarian as beautifully as if they were writing in German. Vörösmarty was the first to simply write in Hungarian without feeling the need for any comparisons.

Generations of women writers are also differentiated in literature. The older women writers adopted male noms de plume and strove to forget they were female when they sat down to their writing desks. Elizabeth Barrett Browning forged the most feminine lyricism into her sonnets with a compact, masculine will. George Eliot wrote like a man.

The younger generation does not harbour such male ambitions. Virginia Woolf says her absolute prerequisite is having *a room of one's own*, where she can be a woman and write without being disturbed. The new women authors, Colette and the great English ladies, write as only women can — and dare — write.

Originally, narrative literature was banter of general interest, linked to specific ceremonies. This ready banter is what gives the ancients their charm; in Homer this is generally ascribed to 'epic exuberance'. Modern women writers give the impression of having slept through the millennia while men were forging their intellects to different ends. These women can still banter away as wonderfully as the Greeks. Reading their work, we cannot for a moment forget that it is a woman we are dealing with. We gently allow her to disclose to us the world she has been living in and towards whose small, secret treasures men have been blinded by their abstractions, their political outlook, their convictions, and the inherent barrenness of male existence. I imagine that for gloomy old bachelors ensconced in their coffee houses the books of Katherine Mansfield could compensate for the more profound humanity that for others is vouchsafed by the psychological presence of women.

From the introduction to the diary I gleaned a great deal about Mansfield's short life. It strikes me as significant that she came to England from New Zealand, the white race's youngest country, which only two hundred years ago was still just a tale borne on the seas. It is true that its first settlers were convicts and other disreputable characters; but Katherine Mansfield was already a fourth-generation New Zealander and with her wonderful freshness a vast new continent has made its contribution to the concert of mankind. Be that as it may, it seems there was in Katherine Mansfield a certain patriotic pride; she wanted to show the world that New Zealand, too, could 'do its bit'. But she does this so modestly and discreetly that without her diary I would never have become aware of the strange country where her childhood stories are set and which I could not, for the life of me, have known to locate on the literary map between Europe and America.

I discovered, furthermore, and not without a pang of distress, that Katherine Mansfield was married to the tedious great English essayist, John Middleton Murry, the one who drew a parallel between Keats and Shakespeare, and in later life devoted himself to Christianity, becoming a kind of English Abbé Bremond. His introduction to her diary suppresses any personal pain and is written with commendable restraint.

It is clear from her diary that Katherine Mansfield could not bear to be constantly in Middleton Murry's company and for much of their marriage they lived apart. *Alors, je pars*, she writes in the diary, which is laced liberally with sentences in French, as Englishwomen always document their learning in such an unsophisticated manner. And then comes this: 'It is astonishing how violently a big branch shakes when a silly little bird has left it. I expect the bird knows it and feels immensely arrogant. The way he went on, my dear, when I said I was going to leave him. He was quite desperate. But now the branch is quiet again. Not a bud has fallen, not a twig has snapped. It stands up in the bright air, steady and firm, and thanks the

Lord that it has got its evenings to itself again'. And later: '*Living alone.* Even if I should, by some awful chance, find a hair upon my bread and honey — at any rate it is my own hair'.

Katherine Mansfield was a casualty of the War. Her younger brother, whom she adored, died on the French front. Grieving for her brother undermined her health, her lungs began to fail, and in 1918 she went to the south of France, her favourite place to stay. But the France of 1918 was no longer what it had been. Even in Paris the food was poor and after grumbling for a while about the breakfasts, she set off homewards. She reached Paris just as the German air raids were beginning and transport was disrupted for weeks on end. These stressful weeks in the capital proved fatal; her tuberculosis became steadily worse and she died in 1923, at the age of only thirty four.

In her diary she writes, for the most part, about things that it would never have occurred to a man to write. Footfalls on the street sound quite different on summer nights. In the room next door a man coughs, she coughs too, and so they commune like two cockerels on unseen farms far from each other. Lodging in unfamiliar hotels, sheltering under the covers, waiting for the shadows to slowly weave their web across the World's Ugliest Wallpaper.

And she complains, as writers do all the time, about her own indolence, about uncomfortable armchairs, that is to say, about the torment of creation. She found it very hard to write. She wrote only if the topic was so alive for her that it came to her involuntarily, in that state Proust spoke of. She envied her husband, who would say: now I'm going to write and wrote until he finished. Poor Katherine Mansfield was not aware how different was the writing of anything scholarly. We read fifty books and then, having thoroughly considered their ideas, take our time writing three hundred pages. A long civilizing process has resulted in essay-writing coming to many as naturally as does thinking (to some). But to write five pages as Katherine Mansfield wrote them — that is a miracle, today just as it was on the first day.

Note to Chapter 10

1. [First published in *Nyugat,* 1 (January 1931).]

CHAPTER 11

Gogol (1944)[I]

What historians of literature marvel at in Gogol is his might as a trail-blazer. In one way or another, every strand of Russian literature can be traced back to him: 'We have all emerged from under Gogol's *Overcoat*,' as Dostoevsky put it. He is the fount of Russia's wonderful realism and its detailed portrayal of ordinary fates: the Dostoevsky of *Poor Folk* and *The Double* is his faithful disciple, while Gogol's quirky sense of humour lives on virtually intact in the work of Ilf and Petrov today. The curious and fascinating lyrical prose, the linguistic and artistic skill represented in our own time by Boris Pilnyak, via Andrei Bely and Aleksey Remizov, had its origins in Gogol's early short stories, just as Russian folk-inspired literature also draws on the same source; indeed, even the Solokhov of *Quiet Flows the Don* follows in the footsteps of Gogol's Cossack heroic epic *Taras Bulba*. Pushkin, Russia's national poet, was Gogol's good friend and mentor; but while Pushkin was respected rather than followed, Gogol was less respected — and yet every writer in Russia learnt something from him, as did very many outside Russia, too.

Gogol died young, knowing nothing of this, and it was no consolation to him in his sickness and ill-fated loneliness.

Nikolai Vasilievich Gogol was born on 31 March 1809 on his father's estate in Velyki Sorochyntsi. His father was a dreamer and a not very practical landowner, whose unfulfilled artistic desires were realized in his son: he is said to have been the model for the sentimental and ineffectual Manilov in *Dead Souls*. As a child Gogol was sickly and rather strange. In Nizhyn his schoolfellows were somewhat wary of him but found him amusing, calling him 'the mysterious dwarf'. He had lofty ambitions from an early age and after completing his education went to St Petersburg to pursue a career in politics. Soon, however, wanderlust got the better of him and he was beguiled by the 'grand tour', intoxicated by the flying troika. He obtained money from his mother in a not entirely gentlemanly way and went to Germany. Then, just as suddenly, he returned home and took up a position in the civil service. His ill-wishers say that for a time he was a member of the notorious Department III, the political police. This would not, in fact, be inconsistent with the overall image we have of him.

His first collection of short stories, *Evenings on a Farm Near Dikanka*, appeared in 1831 and met with immediate acclaim. In 1834 influential patrons helped secure him a post teaching history at St Petersburg University. He gave a number of brilliant lectures on the Middle Ages, but this exhausted the range of his knowledge. In fact, he was ill-prepared for an academic career, a fact of which he was only too aware, and his students, too, must have rapidly reached the same conclusion. One of them was Ivan Turgenev, who recalled him thus:

> To be quite honest, his approach to lecturing was distinctly odd. First of all, if he announced a course of three lectures, he would invariably fail to deliver two of them. Then, on the occasions he did appear in the lecture hall, he would not speak up and just mumbled about this and that in a disjointed manner, showing us steel engravings of Palestine and other Oriental sites. He was in a perpetual state of confusion. We were quite sure he knew nothing at all. At examination time, he appeared with a handkerchief tied around his head and claimed to have toothache. He was a picture of infinite suffering and did not open his mouth. Professor Shulgin conducted the examination in his stead. I can see his thin figure now, with his long nose, and the two corners of his black handkerchief sticking up above his head like ears.

That same year he bade farewell to the department.

Gogol the professor might have failed, but Gogol the writer began his triumphal march the following year: his short-story collection *Mirgorod*, which included the timeless *Taras Bulba*, appeared in 1835. The following year saw the publication of *The Overcoat, The Nose, The Government Inspector*, and it was also about this time that he began *Dead Souls*. The period during which he wrote his greatest works was to last only a few years.

Gogol was not, strictly speaking, Russian but Ukrainian, or Little Russian, or Ruthenian — call him what you will. His homeland, Ukraine, was attached to Russia in 1654; before then it had been partly under Polish suzerainty and partly a 'no man's land' in thrall to the Cossacks. Ukraine today, as I write these lines, is a sizeable plain suffering appallingly from fire and the sword, and the place-names in Gogol's youthful works summon up dreadful mental visions: to say 'Ukraine' is tantamount to saying 'hell'. But in Gogol's time Ukraine was the happiest land in the tsar's vast empire, with bountiful summers succeeding glorious springs, and the Ukrainian people were renowned for their high spirits, songs, dances, and tales. Gogol's early short stories and his first masterpiece, *Taras Bulba*, hark back to those folk and geographical childhood roots. These are folksy writings of a Romantic nature, nurtured on ancient tales and legends, the savage bravery and superstitious fears of the Cossacks of yore.

The masterpieces of his next period, however, are all played out in Greater Russia, that 'something' created out of nothing at Peter the Great's almighty behest, in defiance of the shackles of Russian tradition: the thin lacquer of Europeanization in the empire, the veneer of civilization, with bureaucracy as the driving-force and the *chinovnik*, or middle-rank government official as its most characteristic element. Akaky Akakievich, the hapless hero of *The Overcoat*, is such a *chinovnik*. The theft of his new winter coat, so hard to obtain, killed him. The protagonist in *The Nose* is also this kind of *chinovnik*, who wakes up one morning to find that his nose has run off and is enjoying a splendid career as a brazen fraud. Gogol's immortal *The Government Inspector* is a tragicomedy about Russian bureaucracy as a whole, 'the mocking laughter of the Russian conscience at the Russian state,' as the critic Dmitry Merezhkovsky says. Also a creature of Peter the Great's Russia is the hero of *Dead Souls*, Chichikov, a figure very fussy about his attire, his underwear, his personal hygiene — that is, about everything about himself that he feels to be European. He despises his malodorous peasant servant: his dream is the European dream, the easy and charmed life of the European bourgeoisie.

Ukraine is the past, childhood, the land of fairy tales, while St Petersburg, the Russia of Peter the Great, is the present time, virile adulthood, chequered reality. From out of Gogol the romantic steps Gogol the realist, from soft-hearted, cheerful Gogol the Gogol of the bitter guffaw.

He owes his role in literary history primarily to his realism and humour. He is the founding father and pre-eminent Europe-wide practitioner of that Russian realism of which he is to this day, together with Tolstoy, the greatest master. Gogol himself considered this his most important literary achievement.

'Much has been said about me,' he wrote, 'and attempts have been made to analyse the most varied features of my being, yet all attempts to define my true essence have come to naught. That only Pushkin recognized. He has always said that he had never encountered a writer so able to paint the ordinary and the lacklustre so colourfully, and sketch the general hollowness and insignificance of humankind so forcefully as I.'

By the mid-century realism had become mainstream and writers had generally learnt the vision and techniques that Gogol had felt were unique to himself. But there is something distinctive about Gogol's realism that we look for in vain in Western writers. This something else is truly interesting.

For example, a striking feature of his two chief works of realism, *The Government Inspector* and *Dead Souls*, is that their heroes are not, as in most such works, ordinary folk, but frauds. And Gogol, the accuser and acerbic judge, is not interested in exposing the fraudsters and passing judgement on them; his purpose is to reveal through them the world of honest ordinary people.

To understand this, we need to bear in mind the extraordinary extent to which this great master of realism could revel in dissembling. His contemporaries note that he enjoyed himself most when he was managing to mystify those around him. From their recollections it is clear that he was not generally liked much: 'There was something off-putting about him,' writes Sergei Aksakov, one of his best friends. 'I don't know if anyone liked Gogol as a person. I don't think so; indeed, I consider that impossible.' And the impression we get is more or less that he was not generally liked because people did not know him and to try to do so seemed hopeless. An eccentric and unapproachable personality, he kept well away from those affecting declarations of friendship to which the Russian soul is so peculiarly prone. 'The mysterious dwarf' is what he always remained. He writes: 'There is indeed about me something of Khlestakov' (the fraudster in *The Government Inspector*), and we have no way of knowing whether this was a confession or a boast. He was unknowable and unsettling, unlike the heroes of realist novels — but very like a Gogol character. But here we come to a vicious circle: what is a Gogol character who is unlike the heroes of realist novels *really* like?

Akaky Akakievich is an extremely typical character from a realist novel. However, when his winter coat is stolen and his distress kills him, he turns into a ghost and repeatedly materializes in St Petersburg to appropriate the coats of high-ranking officials. This is how *The Overcoat* ends. Yet had Balzac or Thackeray written it, there would have been no such coda. It is not however just a grotesque, Romantic notion but is of the essence: Akaky Akakievich would have been incomplete if he had not become a ghost. In Gogol, every character carries his own ghost within him. They are the portraits of two devils, said Pushkin of Khlestakov and Chichikov.

It is the cast of Gogol's imagination that makes ghosts of them. He does not invent new lineaments, but hones the existing ones to the point of ghostliness. 'In me everything has moved away from its place,' he writes in one of his letters. 'If, for example, I see someone trip up, my imagination at once appropriates this image and develops it into some dreadful vision, which torments me so much that I am unable to sleep and feel sapped of all my strength.' Here the point is that the most ordinary workaday reality turns ghost-like if we stare at it long and hard enough: one of Gogol's secrets is that he releases the dread that lurks in the workaday. Dostoevsky called Gogol the demon of the guffaw.

Russian literature would seem to run along two adjacent but sharply divergent tracks: the human and the demonic. The human is that of Pushkin, Turgenev, and Tolstoy, the demonic that of Lermontov, Gogol, and Dostoevsky. The human is warm-hearted and enlightened (Tolstoy's religious feeling is characteristically 'enlightened', a critical Christianity that selects only the doctrines that he does not view as counter to common sense). The demonic track, on the other hand, does not believe unconditionally in God (Lermontov could hardly have been much of a believer, and Gogol, as we shall see, only *wanted* to believe) — but it does believe unconditionally in the devil. In *The Brothers Karamazov* the devil appears in person and neither Ivan nor the reader can decide whether this had been Ivan's vision or the Foe himself. And it is strange how this devil's human appearance, his parasitism, and bourgeois ambitions, are so reminiscent of those of Chichikov. In Gogol's works the devil does not put in a personal appearance, but there is all the more discussion of him in them and in Gogol's correspondence. There can be no doubt that for him, even more so than for Dostoevsky, the devil's reality was absolute. He was real — and Gogol feared him.

In Russian intellectual life the Enlightenment developed much later than in other European countries and affected only the narrow stratum of society created by Peter the Great, and even then only to a certain degree; in Gogol's time the vast majority of the population was barely touched by it. In Russia, a world populated by demons and devils, so characteristic of pre-eighteenth century Europe, continued to live on. Russians are much closer to their ancient roots than we in the West are to ours. When Gogol and Dostoevsky feel that the devil is real, they are not strange, deluded souls but identifying far more closely with their people than the westward-looking Turgenev or Tolstoy.

Depending on our perspective of the world this phenomenon can be interpreted in a variety of ways. If we believe unconditionally in progress, we are forced to concede that nineteenth-century Russians and their great, representative writers were sadly backward, and still unaware that demonic forces do not exist. If not unconditional believers in progress, perhaps we might claim that Russians had not yet lost touch with their ancient roots and were *still aware* that demonic forces do exist. At all events, they knew how to depict those forces in a way that made even the most enlightened souls quake in their boots.

And if we pay careful attention to this we will be better able to understand the subsequent, rather enigmatic life of Gogol.

As already mentioned, Gogol began to write his longest and most important work, *Dead Souls*, in 1835, based on an idea and advice from his great friend, Pushkin. Part One appeared in 1842. But for a long time before that, in fact from 1836 onwards, Gogol had been living mainly abroad. He had caught the travel bug, like Turgenev and Dostoevsky later, and he, too, described his homeland's condition from afar. He was spending much of his time in Vevey on Lake Geneva, in Paris, Vienna, Munich, and Baden-Baden, that is to say, in places where at the time high society, particularly that of Russia, congregated — that strange, rootless 'intelligentsia' comprised of the nostalgia-obsessed, peripatetic elite we know so well from Turgenev's novels. Gogol never felt at home anywhere, except in Rome. The holy Eternal City enchanted him and gave him ease. At one point he even considered converting to Catholicism.

But in general he was feeling increasingly unwell. He complained of ever more outlandish and improbable illnesses: for example, he declared to his friends that he had been examined by doctors and found to have a stomach that was upside down. In 1840 in Vienna he had a nervous breakdown. And his great work, *Dead Souls*, did not console him but made him even more desperate.

When he read this work aloud to Pushkin, the latter listened, as always when Gogol was reading to him, with a smile playing about his lips, but then his brow clouded over and he exclaimed: 'God, how sad is our Russia!' And when the work appeared in print Gogol, too, was horrified at the satanic grimace that stared back at him from the pages of his masterpiece: such demonic masks, such a cast of frightening, horrendous Russian characters! He was apologetic: No, Russia was not like this, he said, Russia was great and beautiful and holy, no one knew that better than he. So far he had shown it only in its evil aspects; in the parts of *Dead Souls* still to follow we would be seeing its eternal and peerless face. This was only the *Inferno*, to be followed by the *Purgatorio* and *Paradiso*.

But why are these faces so devilish, he asked himself, stunned, and could find only one answer in his soul: obviously because they were inspired by the devil, who had sprawled over his soul like an over-friendly domestic parasite and was even poking his nose into his work. If he was to be able to write any further parts, he had to exorcise the devil within him. If he wanted to depict good, noble, pure figures, he was going to have to become clean, noble, and good himself. He needed first to redeem himself.

And when he reached this point, writing — art — assumed secondary importance. He, too, like so many other great Russian writers, set greater store by moral than by artistic values, by the soul rather than the mind, and he no longer wanted to portray but to transform and redeem Russia. His entire worldview took an essentially religious turn. Or we might say that from under the thin veneer of

Peter the Great's spirit the true, age-old soul of Russia burst forth and bound his fate with overwhelming force to the Russian community. This turn was also to take place in the lives of Dostoevsky and Tolstoy.

In these circumstances, and for other reasons to be touched upon later, the continuation of *Dead Souls* proceeded very slowly, and instead Gogol wrote another work, no longer applying the techniques of art but appealing directly to the will, explaining what had to be done — urgently, immediately — to stop the devil on his hurtling troika from dragging down with him the whole of holy Russia.

In 1846 he wrote to his publisher as follows: 'Set all other work aside and see to printing this book at once. Its title is *Selections from My Correspondence with Friends*. This is an essential book that everyone needs sorely. For the moment I can say no more: the rest will be made clear to you by the book itself'.

The book appeared in 1847, and it is said that no book ever had a more disastrous reception. It encountered antipathy from readers and critics alike. The two opposing camps of Russian critics, the Westernizers and the Slavophiles, agreed a temporary truce in order to join forces against Gogol. The book met with the approval only of the government and in tsarist Russia no worse publicity for the author than this was conceivable. It was rumoured that Gogol had written it to flatter the highest circles because he wanted to become tutor to the tsarevich.

The most bellicose assault came from the greatest and most dangerous Russian critic, the Westernizers' fearsome leader, Belinsky. By this time Belinsky was already on his deathbed but he wrote that on reading the book he howled in rage like a jackal and forgetting all about his illness immediately set about an excoriating response.[2] This piece is still worth reading today, written as it is with great forcefulness and an exemplary, French-style clarity, and at least in retrospect we must entirely agree with it.

For what Gogol proclaims in this work is that nothing can save Russia short of total submission to the tsar and the Orthodox Church, refraining from unwarranted judgementalism and returning to the patriarchal simplicity of old. But in Russia the 'good old days' meant husbands and fathers horsewhipping their wives and children for the good of their souls. Russia's olden days were not the sun-kissed realms of the European Middle Ages but the rule of Ivan the Terrible, the Tartar hordes, and Stygian gloom. And it seems Gogol was in sympathy with this; it is unnecessary to educate the peasants, he writes: why should they read the empty prattle of westward-looking humanitarians, and in any case they have no time for reading. Belinsky is surely right to say that there is nothing more despicable than to use the sanctity and values of religion to keep ordinary folk permanently in ignorance and oppression.

The one thing that did not occur to Belinsky was that this book had been written by a man pursued by demons, in the terminal crisis of his soul, when he was desperately seeking a way out and, being a Russian, he felt he could escape his demons only collectively, in the company of his own people.

The book's reception totally shattered Gogol. Nobody understood him, nobody. 'I don't know,' he wrote, 'how it is possible that I have not gone mad amid all this appalling chaos. I know only that my heart is broken and I am paralysed. It is impossible to fight raging enemies, but God spare us all from having to fight our friends. If that happens, everything about us falls apart.'

Gogol was not one to stand up heroically against the world on behalf of his ideas. He did not do so because he was not 'steadfast in character' but neither could he have done so because he did not himself believe in these ideas — he only *wanted* to believe in them and that was why he wrote the book. To truly believe in something! As for believing, he really believed only in the devil, all the rest was just an effort to exorcise him, a futile act of self-defence against the devil. He did not stand up for his views, but retracted them apologetically, and even came up with this typically Russian conclusion: 'How fortunate it is that we sometimes receive a public slap in the face ... Perhaps I needed that more than anybody'.

The book failed and Gogol went on fleeing. In 1848 he finally realized a long-standing ambition to make a pilgrimage to Jerusalem so as to seek solace and faith at the Holy Sepulchre. The pilgrimage was a total disaster. He did not find what he had been seeking: 'I must confess,' he wrote in a letter on his way home, 'that I have never been more discontented than in Jerusalem. I saw even more clearly here my selfishness and spiritual aridity'. At the Holy Sepulchre his prayers did not rise heavenwards but only pierced his heart's husk. 'In Nazareth I was caught in the rain and had to stay there two days. It was like waiting in a small railway station in Russia; I did not in the least feel I was in Nazareth.'

These confessions afford those competent in such matters a glimpse into the case history of Gogol's morbid condition. For we consider that even on the evidence of the foregoing there can be no doubt that he was mentally disturbed. Today his illness would probably be diagnosed as schizophrenia, that dreadful illness that has some mysterious bearing on the nature of the creative mind and has been the fate of so many artists. From Gogol's correspondence and the notes concerning him, taken together with his work, certain symptoms of this illness are identifiable as recognized and described by medical science.

It should be said at once that his religiosity is not one of these symptoms. To claim that he suffered from 'religious mania' would be utterly frivolous. I happen to think that there is no such thing; there are only maniacs, some of whom may be religious zealots. It is equally sterile to debate whether his mania was caused by his religiousness or vice versa. Science has not yet identified the causes of schizophrenia. Gogol's religion is linked to his illness only in that he fruitlessly sought in it an escape and a cure.

The most typical symptom of schizophrenia is what in more technical language is called the 'progressive impoverishment of the personality'. This characterized his experiences, or rather, his non-experiences, in Nazareth and Jerusalem. Other excerpts from his letters suggest that Gogol felt incapable of feeling anything and that something inside him was dying or perhaps had already died. Gradually he was overwhelmed by an enormous sense of gloom, interested in nothing, and feeling totally unconnected. Vast expanses of ice lay between himself and the world. He was shrouded in a great, cosmic loneliness. 'If just one human being were willing to speak to me! It's as if everything had died. As if there were only dead souls in Russia. It's horrendous, horrendous.'

And this is why he could not write at all, or only in those rare hours when the surface of the ice yielded somewhat, and even then only very little.

And in his loneliness the ghosts burst in on him.

There are two kinds of ghost. One is the 'animistic' ghost, the spirit freed of its mortal coil. The other, more ancient, is the 'pre-animistic' ghost, the 'living dead', deprived of a soul but able to come and go, zombie-like. Gogol sometimes sees his fellow men as living corpses: 'It shrivels my soul,' he wrote, 'to see how many silent, dead people are walking the world, and how dreadful is the stony iciness of their souls'. At other times it is himself he describes: 'I swear my situation is sometimes as desperate as that of the living dead, who watch themselves being buried, yet cannot raise a finger or give any sign that they are still alive'.

In this light the title of his masterwork acquires a new meaning. In Gogol's time *Dead Souls* referred to dead serfs: it was an accepted technical term and this is the sense in which Gogol used it in his novel. But to anyone unacquainted with this work its title suggests something quite different: there is some unspeakable dread lurking in it. This is what the censor, a person of simple faith, must have felt when he did not want to let through a novel bearing such a title: there are no dead souls, he reasoned, for our Church teaches that the soul is immortal. Dead souls do not exist, but here are souls that are alive yet behave as if they were dead... Gogol chose the technical term as his title but it is impossible that, consciously or not, he could have failed to take into account the other sense of the expression as well. His deeper intuition must have anticipated that he would himself be a dead soul.

And now only the final act remains.

Returning from the Holy Land Gogol made the acquaintance of a monk called Father Matthew, in whom he saw his last chance to escape. About this Father Matthew Gogol's biographers, even those religiously inclined, have only disagreeable things to say. He was a fanatical, hard-hearted, ruthless priest who possessed no knowledge of the human soul and was far too unsophisticated to appreciate the complexity of Gogol's character. For a fragile patient he prescribed a drastic cure and killed him. But it must be granted that Father Matthew, precisely because he was a primitive monolithic personality, represented something that Gogol had been seeking all his life: the ancient, simple, yet majestic folk faith of the Russians. In his warped and brutish way he was a prefiguration of the holy peasants of Tolstoy and Dostoevsky.

Father Matthew was an either-or man. Either we live for the world, or we live for Christ. And if we live for Christ we must give up all life's vanities. And if we do not, then nothing can save us from the devil — yes, the devil, and the torments of hell, which Father Matthew was able to delineate with a flair for folk realism. Even if he had deliberately sought him out, Gogol could not have found himself more fatal company.

Writing, too, was one of the proscribed worldly vanities. Against this Gogol protested most vehemently. If I do not write, then I do not live, he argued in a final outburst of sanity. The struggle was extremely protracted, but it ended with the triumph of the stronger will.

Of the second part of *Dead Souls* only a brief fragment saw the light of day, thanks to a manuscript that happened to survive Gogol's death. But it is likely that Gogol had written more than that and had perhaps even finished it. The manuscript of the completed work was destroyed.

On the night of 11 February 1852 Gogol had been praying with even greater zeal than usual. He then stood up, summoned his servant, and candle in hand passed through his rooms, making the sign of the Cross in each. Suddenly he took out a bundle of manuscript and threw a large part into the fireplace, setting it ablaze with his candle. The servant seemed to grasp what was happening and with tears in his eyes begged him to spare the papers. 'No business of yours,' retorted Gogol, 'get on with your praying!' He waited until the pile had turned to ashes, crossed himself, kissed his servant in the Russian manner, returned to his bedroom and, throwing himself on his bed, burst into tears.

Strangely enough, even then his predilection for mystification did not leave him. The following day he recounted the story to his friend, Count A. P. Tolstoy, in whose house he had once lived, as follows: 'Just imagine how powerful the Evil One is! I wanted to burn some manuscripts I no longer needed and instead I threw on the fire the chapters of *Dead Souls* I had wanted to bequeath to my friends to remember me by'.

After this he lived for only a short time. For a long time previously he had been fasting a great deal and mortifying his flesh. Now he stopped eating altogether. He consumed only wafers and also deprived himself of sleep. When he was reduced to a shadow of his former self and his organs were beginning to fail, doctors were called. Their diagnosis was gastroenteritis caused by exhaustion. Leeches were applied to his body, he was made to sit in boiling water, had cold water poured over his head, he was made to drink bitter infusions, and finally plastered with slices of hot bread. The only thing they did not think to give him was something to eat. On 21 February 1852 Gogol starved to death.

His last words were: 'The ladder... the ladder!' Perhaps he was thinking of the Mystic Ladder that might have enabled him to climb out of the devil's clutches and which he had vainly searched for his whole life long.

Notes to Chapter 11

1. [First published in *Magyar csillag*, 4 (15 February 1944).]
2. [Vissarion Belinsky, letter to N. V. Gogol, 3 July 1847, first published by A. I. Herzen in *The Polar Star* in 1855 (2nd edn (London, 1858), pp. 66–76).]

CHAPTER 12

Marcel Proust (1936)[I]

In the renaissance of the novel, especially the revolutionary French novel, every stream converges into this one name, the name of this man who was so ill that he did not live to see the publication of his novel in full and now contemplates with the detachment of the departed how his work has gone on to conquer the world.

Proust was comfortably off, a sophisticated man of leisure whose life was filled with gossip and the social round. In his final years problems with his heart and nerves turned him into a recluse. He spent his days in a cork-lined room with the curtains drawn, completely shutting out the world, the world he had previously lived for: *le monde*, in the elegant, societal sense of the French word. It was in these years that he composed his *À la recherche du temps perdu*. He is said to have continued to work on this until the last moments of his life; even as he lay on his deathbed he asked for the manuscript to be brought to him because he wanted to revise some detail in its description of the death agony. Thus, as he was unable to make major changes, the work reached the public in a form that was unpolished yet perhaps all the more suited to his nature, the first volume appearing in 1913, the remainder between 1923 and 1927.

À la recherche du temps perdu, in search of lost time. The title means, among other things, that the book is autobiographical. But it also means much more than this. There resounds in it its basic motif, the tolling of lost time, of time itself....

All novels have this as their theme: a specific time-span filled with the events recounted and which establish a particular rhythm making it into experiential time in the human sense, time being a sequence of changes. The raw material of both being action, time and the novel are inseparable. Hence the philosophical problem of the novel is always the writer's treatment of time. In the history of the novel every major turning point leads necessarily to a change in the perception of time, and vice versa.

The traditional novel is based on the traditional conception of time. Minutes follow minutes, years follow years, with a minute lasting exactly a minute and a year exactly a year. This is the time-span that is signalled mechanically by the clock and the calendar. It was Bergson who pointed out that actual duration, the time that we experience in the soul's own reality, is something quite different. Actual duration is measured in accordance with the content of our experience. There are days that are so uneventful that their actual duration is zero. Moreover, reality time does not always follow a chronological sequence. There are moments that occur later in the mind than what follows them in clock time.

This time concept, Bergson's *durée réelle*, is evident in Proust. In his work a description of events and situations of only a moment's duration sometimes takes up a hundred pages, while elsewhere years are disposed of in a single sentence. What he records, and seeks, is not mechanical time, but 'reality time'.

Reality time, according to Proust, exists outside actuality as ordinarily understood. It exists only in the soul or, to be more precise, in memory. It is memory that is, properly speaking, life. Nothing is beautiful or ugly in itself. Only in the mind does it become like something or other, by virtue of the fact that it recalls something. One of his heroes, Swann, is passionately in love with his wife because she recalls a Botticelli painting. When the narrator's beloved grandmother dies, he is unable to feel truly sad; only years later, when memory conjures up his grandmother's figure, is he able to shed true tears.

This memory of which Proust speaks is not the mechanical recall through thought, always at the disposal of us all, and which, even then, reproduces only an even fainter copy of a faint reality. There is another, involuntary memory, and it is this that Proust means.

This kind of memory generally breaks in upon us unexpectedly, quite independently of our will. Proust thinks it gets conjured into objects, like spirits in ancient tales, and it is we who set it free. He tells how once a taste of a certain delicacy, a madeleine, such as he used to eat as a child, flooded him with memories. 'No sooner had the warm liquid mixed with the crumbs touched my palate than a shudder ran through me and I stopped, intent upon the extraordinary thing that was happening to me. An exquisite pleasure had invaded my senses, something isolated, detached, with no suggestion of its origin. And at once the vicissitudes of life had become indifferent to me, its disasters innocuous, its brevity illusory'.[2] Because it was at that moment that childhood became for him a segment of lost time, life in its reality.

When 'in reality' a child, his life, like everyone else's, was fragmented into a thousand minute impressions and did not have for him the same intensity as when, in the miracle of remembrance, all of his entire childhood, everything comprising the essence of childhood, appeared to him. It is only in such moments of remembrance that we are truly alive. And he devotes the first volume of the novel to an exhaustive analysis of all that was contained in that single moment when he tasted the madeleine he dipped into his tea.

A moment such as this offers the only happiness on this earth. Proust, too, is a Vitalist, like almost all the new novelists. But for him what is generally called life is not truly life. Our ambitions, friendships, loves are so shot through with illusory and confusing moments that do not occasion genuine joy and do not bring about in us the sensation of life in all its intensity. It is only when we conjure forth from objects the soul that they harbour deep within them, which is our own soul, an entire period belonging to our soul that is already over and gone — it is only then we remember that we are truly alive. Those are the minutes that it is incumbent on the writer to record; in this consists the search for lost time.

In discovering lost time Proust's greatest help is his incomparable sensibility. Just as he has the ability to experience in a single moment entire swathes of his life, he is also capable, aided by an even rarer faculty of the spirit, of experiencing in a single moment the thousand nuances and import of a gesture or an object. Matters we are not ordinarily conscious of noticing, and at best register on a subconscious level, elicit from Proust such a powerful and exuberant reaction that he can devote page after page to analysing the nuances of his feelings.

It might be a gesture: he observes the intimate niceties of a greeting and describes them in the minutest detail — and it is from things such as this that he constructs his monumental panorama of society. An object (he is moved primarily by objects), such as the church spires of Martinville viewed from his carriage, elicits from him different emotions at different points along the way; it is this experience that awakens in him the desire to be a writer, so as to give an account of the feelings aroused by the objects. He feels as though every object has some mysterious meaning that is merely waiting to be liberated by his pen. When his carriage passes a clump of trees without his having perceived their secret meaning, Proust writes: 'I was as wretched as if I had just lost a friend, had died myself, had broken faith with the dead or repudiated a god'.[3]

Or a name: Proust is a man of history, his inner life is steeped in history and people and objects, but it is above all names that resonate in him, echoing far back into the centuries. Thus, for example, the name Guermantes, borne in the novel by the family that stands on the highest rung of the social ladder, embodied above all in the beautiful Oriana, duchesse de Guermantes, of whom Proust writes that she was 'invariably wrapped in the mystery of the Merovingian age, and bathed, as in a sunset, in the amber light which glowed from the resounding syllable: "antes"'.[4]

Maybe there exists some other person, somewhere, in whom impressions surface with such a miraculous richness of nuance; but there was no one before Proust with the capacity for creating an awareness of them and giving them expression to such a degree. This richness of nuance also exists in us, Proust's readers and devotees; if it did not, we should be unable to understand him and engage emotionally with him. But in us these impressions remain below the threshold of awareness — until they are liberated by Proust. Proust's most wonderful attribute was that in him no sharp division existed between the conscious and the unconscious, as if in the mechanism of his intellect the trapdoor, whose function was in practice to exclude associations of ideas 'surplus to requirements' in daily life, failed to function properly: every association slipped into his conscious with ease. A sensibility such as this comes our way perhaps once in a century, if at all. He truly fulfilled the desire of Novalis: he dreamt awake and was awake in his dreams; things conscious and unconscious achieved unity in him, interpenetrating each other.

By claiming that someone like this comes our way once in a hundred years, we are also saying that Proust was a 'special', pathological soul. A surfeit of sensibility is just as 'abnormal' as an insufficiency of it. In him the hypersensitivity of the neurotic, usually only an attribute of the spirit, became a creative facility of the intellect. He was all too aware of this himself, writing of 'the splendid and pitiable family [sc. of neurotics] which is the salt of the earth'.[5] And his circumstances served to amplify his abilities. Others are obliged to use their intellectual capacity for practical purposes and push the vast majority of their associations and impressions into their subconscious because they obstruct free movement. Proust's wealth relieved him of the pressures of life's practicalities and in concert with his illness, which enforced isolation upon him, accustomed him to fathoming the depths of everything that welled up in his subconscious at a leisurely pace and with fanatical thoroughness. In this sense he was right that what makes great artists creative is sickness and suffering; health and happiness are not productive.

From the foregoing it follows that his narrative technique consists not in the registration of facts but in analysis. He recounts an event not ordinarily significant in itself: some girls coming towards him along the seafront, bringing to the duc de Guermantes news that a relative of his has died, and so forth. To this Proust adds his commentary, those associations of his which, as we have said, he develops with obsessional precision. He constructs this edifice regardless of any kind of practical consideration or novelistic interest. He may perhaps in a single sentence skate over a matter generally of interest to novel-readers and linger page after page over less interesting elements, perhaps of a kind not even the most reverential Proust-devotee can comprehend.

If we re-read Proust now, at a decade's distance from the enthusiasm with which we first read him, we have to concede that he is really dreadfully verbose. His book is full of the most splendid thoughts, but he relates those splendid thoughts over and over again, varying them endlessly, like a musical motif run wild. On a first reading we do not notice this, because the thoughts are novel and it is through their repetition that we understand them better. But nothing loses its gloss so quickly as a thought, and today we would prefer Proust to have committed each to paper once only; even so, many would now sound like trite, self-evident truisms.

But what remains in all its magnificent inviolability is the portrayal, the depiction that constitutes Proustian art. Materialized in his *oeuvre* is the principle of 'interpenetration' proclaimed by Walter Pater as the highest requisite of art: the total reciprocal interpenetration of the internal and external worlds. The physical object, the spiritual experience occasioned by it, and the intellectual content associated with the experience meld in a threefold unity. Intellectual content is included, for as a writer Proust is not merely a conjurer of life out of objects and the century's finest portrayer of the soul, he is also a *Kulturschriftsteller*. His vast trove of cultural knowledge is embedded in his novel. This culture is not cumbrous ballast in the body of the novel but a symptom of those intellectual good manners of which he speaks at one point: recognition of the fact that cultural experiences are just as organic a part of the life of today's cultured person as impressions elicited by objects. For members of the cultural elite, such as the book's hero and those to whom the book is primarily addressed, it is history that provides life's most enduring and emotionally enriching backdrop.

So much for the book's technique. As for its theme: Proust attempts to offer, like Balzac, a comprehensive cross-section of French life, a *tableau des mœurs*; the book is a summation of life in pre-war, wartime, and immediately post-War France. In its portrayal of society, too, it surpasses its antecedents. The latter for the most part conceived of society as the sum total of individual lives and strove to present social communities through the lives of typical individuals. None of those had such feel for exactly what is social about society, that is to say, for social (rather than emotional) relationships. His predecessors showed how a typical representative of a particular social class reacted to abiding supra-societal issues such as love, poverty, and death. What concerns Proust, however, is how a member of society reacts to society itself, how he tries to find his place in it, and what bearing such a striving, such an encounter with the frictions engendered by society, has on his character and fate.

Nor does he stop at presenting the individual classes in isolation; he splendidly analyses the relationship of the classes to each other. His speciality is what might be called the comparativist critique of society: how the aristocrat responds to the simple man, what the *haut bourgeois* thinks of the aristocrat, how one class merges into another — these are the skills in which Proust is a virtuoso.

In Proust's summation every social class has its proper place and as he has all his characters speak with the accuracy of a recording in the register of their particular class, his work conserves, museum-like, the speech inflections of pre-War France. None the less, one class in particular and its fate lies at the heart of the novel, and that class is the aristocracy.

Odd as it may sound it was Proust who discovered the aristocracy for the art of the novel. Virtually not since Saint-Simon had anyone written about aristocrats. (In England there was one such writer in the nineteenth century, Disraeli, who was later prime minister, and in France, to an extent, Paul Bourget.) While there are to this day very many books and plays ostensibly about aristocratic persons, the counts and dukes in these are counts and dukes only in the way that the Greeks of French classical theatre are Greek. For the most part the aristocratic environment features in literature only in a negative sense: it means that the novel or play is not set in a bourgeois or folk milieu and the author is therefore relieved of the obligation to spend much time on the presentation of the milieu itself and can instead devote all his energies to 'ordinary people', as was the case when the French classical authors wrote of Greeks or Turks. But they could not present the aristocracy as a milieu, as a reality, if only because as a rule they knew nothing about it.

It is a cardinal truth of literary sociology that social classes become a theme of literature only when they begin to decline. Proust, too, came on the scene at the last moment, when the world of the Faubourg St Germain stood on the brink of destruction. It was not that the French aristocracy had died out during the War — something far more terminal happened: it had opened its doors to ordinary folk, losing its exclusivity and ceasing to be a rigidly closed class. It is this process of disintegration and decay that Proust documents in his novel.

The paramount longing of the novel's hero, from childhood onwards, is to gain an entry into aristocratic society, in particular, to be able to circulate in the salons of the fabled historical Guermantes family. The novel's hero is thus a snob; this is undeniable, nor would Proust deny it for a moment. Snobbery is one of those sentiments that were a taboo topic for the democratically-inclined literature of the nineteenth century, in the same way as Romanticism made the love of money, along with the passions and proclivities that go with it, into a taboo. Even if snobs and social climbers did make an appearance, it was as obnoxious schemers or comic bystanders. Proust rehabilitated snobbery, that powerful passion of the *ancien régime*.

Proust does not claim that snobbery is a morally estimable quality — but then he generally refrains from passing moral judgements. He avers only that this is a passion that exists in the world, that for very many it is the most powerful of passions, the life-affirming centre of their personality, hence it is an object he deems worthy of scrutiny. His novel is a thoroughgoing natural history of snobbery, a wide-ranging exploration of it in all its manifestations.

Proust held that the purpose of art was perception. Yet there exist phenomena that are too complex and subtle to be amenable to a scientific approach — they are so slight and slithery that they slip through the net of rational perception. Of such phenomena we can be made aware only through art, aided by intuition. Most phenomena of spiritual life are of this nature.

We are today no longer as sure as we were twenty years ago that the world and mankind are making progress. But we can be certain that knowledge of the soul has grown over the centuries; this is one respect in which we indubitably differ from the Greeks or the Elizabethans. Shakespeare was one of the greatest of poets — yet any run-of-the-mill novelist today knows more, and in more detail, about the life of the soul.

Science has not been the means whereby we have attained knowledge of the soul. Psychology as a science is still in its infancy and flees in alarm from the extreme complexities of psychological phenomena, escaping into the diversions of experimental psychology or the no less jejune oversimplifications of psychoanalysis. Our knowledge of the soul has been acquired primarily through literature and, above all, through the novel. One of the most significant and glorious milestones on the path of this development is the *oeuvre* of Marcel Proust.

Notes to Chapter 12

1. [First published in Antal Szerb, *Hétköznapok és csodák* (Budapest: Révai, 1936).]
2. [Marcel Proust, *Remembrance of Things Past: Swann's Way*, trans. by C. K. Scott Moncrieff and Terence Kilmartin (London: Chatto and Windus, 1981), I, p. 48 ('Mais à l'instant même où la gorgée mêlée des miettes du gâteau toucha mon palais, je tressaillis, attentif à ce qui se passait d'extraordinaire en moi. Un plaisir délicieux m'avait envahi, isolé, sans la notion de sa cause. Il m'avait aussitôt rendu les vicissitudes de la vie indifférentes, ses désastres inoffensifs, sa brièveté illusoire').]
3. [Proust, *Remembrance of Things Past: Within a Budding Grove*, trans. by C. K. Scott Moncrieff and Terence Kilmartin (New York: Random House, 1981), I, p. 773 ('J'étais triste comme si je venais de perdre un ami, de mourir moi-même, de renier un mort ou de méconnaître un dieu').]
4. [Proust, *Remembrance of Things Past: Swann's Way*, trans. by C. K. Scott Moncrieff and Terence Kilmartin (New York: Random House, 1981), I, p. 187 ('[t]oujours enveloppée du mystère des temps mérovingiens et baignant comme dans un coucher de soleil dans la lumière orangée qui émane de cette syllabe: *antes*').]
5. [Proust, *Remembrance of Things Past: The Guermantes Way* (London: Chatto and Windus, 1981), II, p. 315 ('cette famille magnifique et lamentable qui est le sel de la terre').]

CHAPTER 13

Thomas Mann (1936)[1]

Like Marcel Proust, Thomas Mann deserves a chapter to himself; they are the two greatest writers of the age. Like Proust, Mann is a lone peak, without kith or kin in the history of the novel.

Thomas Mann's first writings date from well before the outbreak of the War. In his *Buddenbrooks* (1901) he produced German Naturalism's greatest and perhaps only enduring novel, and the small-scale short story form achieved a perfection in his depiction of the soul that surpassed its Russian and Scandinavian models. He was the greatest master of a style that became obsolete with the War and against which every modern novel is a reaction. However, for Thomas Mann the perfection of his own work was not enough. The nature of his surprising, protean sea-change, his evolution, is perhaps his only characteristically German trait. This he has in common with his German contemporary, Gerhart Hauptmann.

The transformation and evolution away from Naturalism takes place before the reader's very eyes in *Der Zauberberg* (*The Magic Mountain*), which the novelist published in 1924 after a long period of silence.

At the outset *Der Zauberberg* adopts the tools of that minor art form, the Naturalist novel; it begins with an extraordinarily detailed and precise description of the life of consumptives in a sanatorium, of the states of mind resulting from a raised temperature. When he began the novel Mann perhaps intended to do no more than offer a portrait of a society marginalized by this disease — his imagination was always drawn to the triumph of sickness and decay. But as he progressed there appeared by the sickbed of Hans Castorp, his youthful everyman (a typical hero of a Naturalist novel) two symbolic figures, representatives of the prewar world's two main intellectual forces: Settembrini, or rationalist humanism, and Naphta, or a paradoxical Romantic neo-piety, and the battle of the angels for the soul of the German youth commenced.

In accordance with its internal gigantomachy, the story gradually began to gain in intricacy, and the naturalistic observation of the thermometer was ousted by the props of the Romantic novel: secret loves, mysterious human generosity (Mynheer Peeperkorn), duels, suicides, death, and necromancy, and by the final chapters the figure of Hans Castorp has dissolved into a collectivity advancing blindly and with feverish trembling towards the War.

Der Zauberberg is an all-encompassing novel, indeed a novel that encompasses that greatest of totalities, the totality of the intellect. In the form of conversations and monologues it raises all those issues of utmost importance that exercised the pre-War elite and that still remain unresolved. The rich texture of its thought completely dwarfs the work of the younger intellectual novelists, such as Aldous Huxley. This is a truly encyclopedic book.

And a novel notwithstanding! That, from the artistic point of view, is the most miraculous and mysterious thing about it. There is no other novel whose boundaries shade so imperceptibly into the essay as those of *Der Zauberberg*. And not the light, English type either, but the heavy, philosophical German essay, in which Georg Simmel, György Lukács, and Max Scheler are past masters. And yet in these essay-inserts it is not the author speaking but the wonderfully lively characters, infused by him with rhythm and dynamism, so that through them two opponents each have their say, and every topic we are presented with is illuminated from both sides, rationality and irrational ultra-rationality. In this antithetical form perhaps a fundamental characteristic of the German spirit finds expression, the fateful and, from the intellectual standpoint, truly splendid gift of polarization, an *a priori* duality, viewing everything from two opposing sides. *Alles ist gerade und alles ist ungerade*, everything is straight and everything is not straight, as Goethe said.

The novel does not, of course, consist solely of conversations. From the point of view of the formal requirements of the novel, too, it is quite outstanding in terms of the astonishing plasticity of the characters, its wealth of delicate psychological detail, and the convincing nature of the mysterious interconnections in the web of loves and friendships, all so full of life. Despite a thousand characters and issues it is elevated into an integral whole by its omnipresent basic motif and, with its revelatory originality and those qualities of a loftier modernity and of total timelessness with which only the very greatest are endowed, casts a spell more powerful than any sensational tale. Why? Because this novel is the battleground of powers more dread than any: of life and death, in the abstract and therefore the strictest sense of the words.

The core of the new novel's outlook on life, its *Weltanschauung* was, as we have seen, Vitalism, the struggle for the new, Nietzschean 'tablets of stone', which ascribe the highest value to the fullness of life. From the ideological, philosophical point of view the Germans are born one stage higher than the children of others, which the English acknowledge to this day by using the German word *Weltanschauung* to denote the concept of ideology. For this reason, in the German novel Vitalism never assumed such naive forms as in the English (D. H. Lawrence) and the American. And it is natural, too, for the greatest novelist in the German-speaking world to profess as his outlook on life a form of Vitalism that is more profound, critical, and comprehensive than that of the others.

The primitive tenet of Vitalism — that the greatest value is life — has a natural though often unarticulated corollary, that the greatest evil is death. Rigid conventions are the dead trappings of social life, moral inhibitions are the mortal coils of a now lifeless faith. The greyness of bourgeois existence springs from passions suppressed by artificial means, thus it, too, is the outcome of death. The Vitalist finds himself confronting death at every turn and digs himself a shelter against it. His goal is the moment intensified beyond all measure: ecstasy, which breaks out of time and transience.

Yes, but: *alles ist gerade und alles ist ungerade*. Mann recognized that no one who fully avows life can entirely disavow death, because death is integral to life in the way (say) that form is to content. He speaks of the two alternative figures of Hans Castorp's grandfather: the living one had been a doddery old gentleman, the dead one, lying on his catafalque, a powerful patrician of symbolic magnitude.

Death has the advantage over life. Death is form, life chaos; death is clean, life is in unclean ferment; death is enduring, life transient. Our moral and intellectual ideals all strive towards the cleanness of death. Death is spirit, life is matter. Therefore, from those two, to choose only life is to renounce everything in life of a higher order and thereby impoverish life itself — to such an extent that the Vitalist extremist is self-contradictory, because no one who disavows death can achieve fullness of life.

But there are other reasons, too, to be unable to achieve the fullness of life. Death is embedded in life not just as its corollary but as a positive life value. The instinct that draws the spirit towards death is the twin of the life instinct and has the same power. Rapture — part fleshly, part spiritual — of identical intensity serves as a lure on the sides of both the life and the death instinct. In fact, the two cannot be clearly separated. At life's highest, most intense moments, in ecstasy, there is always present, alongside the rapture of life's plenitude, the sweetness of death, without which the feeling of being alive would be incomplete. As a matter of fact the Greek term for ecstasy means that at such times the soul leaves life, it disintegrates, spills over into something else; it is destroyed, consumed. Not to experience that annihilation is not to know life's fullness. As Goethe wrote:

> And until you know of this:
> How to grow through death
> You're just another troubled guest
> On the gloomy earth.[2]

Without the sweetness of death, the sweetness of life is not genuine. And sometimes death's sweetness exerts a far stronger magnetic pull on the spirit than that of life. A battle between angels, that of life and death, takes place in the soul. How many sick people die because the call of death is the stronger? But it is not only sick people: anyone who has striven to rise above the workaday world (and it is perhaps such a person who is ill, so far as society is concerned) can already hear within the two angels' battle cries. Hans Castorp, too, when raised above his humdrum daily existence by the enforced meditations of sanatorium life and the ideologies wrestling for his allegiance discovers in his soul the siren calls of death. He gets lost on a skiing trip; tired, he falls asleep, and then, on the verge of freezing to death, as he dreams, that is to say, instinctively, he must choose between life and death. It would be easier and sweeter to go on sleeping, freeze, and die. But his dreaming state reveals to him a way through the moving and piteous history of humankind towards something better, and he awakens, pulls himself together, and chooses life, not because to live is better than to die, but because of goodness and love for others, for humanity.

This is an antithetical version of Vitalism, that views simultaneously both sides. Compared with this approach, which reconciles opposites, how rudimentary is the life-cult of others!

Already in his first great work, *Buddenbrooks*, Thoman Mann had made his debut as a decadent writer. Its subject matter, a patrician family's slow decline, was especially suitable for conveying the mood of decadence so fashionable at the time. In most of his subsequent work it is evident that he is attracted to illness, decline, and decay, and how strong a pull the sweetness of death exerts on him. In *Der Zauberberg*, however, decadence is no longer a matter merely of the spirit of the age, nor an individual disposition, but an act of perception born of the creative process. This is not a destructive but a constructive force, enabling Mann to complement Vitalism, and the result is perhaps the most significant psychological discovery of our time.

Art is perception. Thomas Mann, exactly like Marcel Proust, acquired knowledge in essential matters not through any scientific study but, by using artistic intuition and his own uncompromisingly honest self-observation, stole a march on science and discovered new continents. Psychology has so far taken only very tentative steps towards uncovering the role of the death instinct in the life of the individual and the community, notably in the later works of Freud. But for the moment this entire field of the study of the soul remains eerily mysterious. Probably even today we do not fully understand *Der Zauberberg*, as through it we take cognizance of matters mainly, so far as we are concerned, still shrouded in the veil of the unconscious. In this respect *Der Zauberberg* has a prophetic character and what it has to say will only be revealed in its entirety at a later stage of humanity's awareness.

To quote a favourite expression of the philosopher Ákos Pauler, Vitalism 'leads beyond itself'. It leads over out of life and into its own negation, into death. And it leads beyond in another sense as well: in order not to deny itself after all, it is obliged to summon to its aid another, older, non-Vitalistic set of values. It is not because it is better to live but out of goodness and love for humankind, that is to say, out of humanism, that Hans Castorp chooses life. Vitalism becomes imbued with meaning only when it is morally complemented by humanism.

For Mann is a believer in humanism. He is a fanatic believer in good old, prewar humanism, even if events and the spirit of the age are determinedly against him. In his theoretical work he always promulgated humanism; it is their humanity that brings his novels close to our hearts, and it was for the sake of his humanism that he accepted the bitter fruit of exile in his final years. There is nothing sentimental about his humanism, and little compassion; his is not the humanism of Dickens or Gerhart Hauptmann. It is a chilly humanism, one that jibes well with irony and quiet disdain for the man in the street.

This is humanism not as a feeling but as an attitude to life; in practice it is primarily a negative stance: abhorrence of the use of force, of tyranny, of the crippling of individuality. This is the humanism of the eighteenth century, of Voltaire and Goethe. It derives from an awareness of human dignity, and from the intellectual's serenity, tenderness, and horror of fighting, for it rises far, far above the passions that provoke human beings to commit bloody barbarities. It is an ethos that is not rooted in any feeling or religion, but solely and uniquely in the intellect. This intellect-based morality has been from Goethe onwards the greatest pride and achievement of the German spirit, and from this the new

German world, with its new uncertainty in ethics and intuitions, has diverged the furthest.

After *Die Zauberberg* the artist took his ease with two short novels in his earlier, naturalistic mode: *Unordnung und frühes Leid* (*Disorder and Early Sorrow*), a vivid, perfectly articulated portrait of life in post-War Germany, and *Mario und der Zauberer* (*Mario and the Magician*), an allegorical account of life in Mussolini's Italy that found it sorely wanting.

These were followed by another great work. Of his Bible-themed trilogy two volumes have appeared so far: *Die Geschichten Jaakobs* (*The Tales of Jacob*) and *Joseph und seine Brüder* (*Joseph and his Brothers*).[3]

When Mann's admirers first opened *Die Geschichten Jaakobs*, their first reaction was generally shock. The book begins with a wholly abstract introduction of 150 pages and what follows, a 100-page dialogue between Jacob and Joseph, seems no more enthralling. But what most shocks the reader is the question: what is the maestro's purpose with this topic that is really rather remote from the present-day world?

Mann clearly did not intend this book as easy poolside reading and perhaps the heavy introduction was intended to scare off the hoi polloi. But, however improper it may be to recommend such a course, the impatient reader can skip the introduction without compunction, and once over the initial shock, will enjoy the novel. And can then even read it by the pool.

The central element of Mann's literary art has always been irony, of a kind, paradoxically, consistent with respect for the very thing that it mocks; indeed, it is often an expression of affection. This is an irony not of destruction but perception-based. *Alles ist gerade und alles ist ungerade.* That which we truly perceive loses its hazy and contourless splendour, coaxes from us a friendly smile, and in it we catch a glimpse of the grotesque latent in all things while, however, simultaneously also discovering in it that intimate splendour which, humanly, is more valuable than anything else. It is with that irony born of perception that Thomas Mann turns towards myth, in the form of the Bible Story, one of the myths that Europeans have in common.

An important aspect of the post-War temper is that interest in myth grew by leaps and bounds. The history of religion, previously a scholarly specialism, now became the favourite preoccupation of the intellectual elite. There was a gradual dawning of recognition that myth is not, as the Enlightenment thought, a poetic artifice or, as the history of religion taught, a priestly fabrication, nor even the expression of some immemorial need of the human spirit, but something more: one of the most splendid embodiments of perception. There are facts concerning the world apprehensible only in the form of myth. Ages with no mythology of their own are impoverished ages, as they lack knowledge of these truths.

The new dignity of myth is a phenomenon contemporary with and parallel to the new turn in the novel, with its return to pure fiction, to wonders. Wonders, too, belong to the realm of mythical perception. The new novelists are permanently preoccupied with myth. D. H. Lawrence and J. C. Powys attempt to create new mythologies of their own; others, like the German Hans-Friedrich Blunck for example, reach back into the mythic world of their nation; and Greek myth, too, has once again come to the fore since Carl Spitteler. From the point of view of intellectual history it is not at all surprising that the two most distinguished representatives of the great generation of Germans, Thomas Mann and Gerhart Hauptmann, almost simultaneously turned towards myth. They wanted to satisfy the most profound intellectual demands of the European elite.

Mann's approach to myth is, as we have said, of an ironic character. He wanted to get behind myth, to show what had happened in actual fact. This is a very dangerous attitude, which threatens to offer the cheap, lackey-like, revelatory *Schadenfreude* of the Enlightenment, of which not even Anatole France was entirely free. But Mann's irony is of a higher order, interested not in revelations but in perception, fostered by examining everything from both sides at once. It is perhaps here that this manner of seeing things achieves its highest expression in literature.

Let us, for example, look at Jacob through Mann's eyes. From one angle Jacob is a crafty old Jew, adept at couching his rapacity and unjust partiality towards Joseph in grand mythological imagery. The other shows him as a man of God who, aided by the mystical experience of God that resides within him, humanizes the hitherto barbaric religious and moral life of his people. The most enormous oppositions meld in the human soul. Jacob almost dies because of the news that Joseph is lost, but at the same time histrionically ensures that the expression of his suffering should be as effective as possible. Genuine and counterfeit feelings are inseparably mingled in the soul. About the soul's falsity, this outstanding discovery in the psychology of the new novel, it is Mann who, alongside Proust and Huxley, has the most pertinent things to say.

All mythology is such a double-edged business. Humankind makes myth but subsequently myth makes humankind. Jacob and his sons were clear about their mythic roles and remained faithful to them. They give the name Eliezer to Jacob's old chief servant, just as they had to Abraham's, and this Eliezer gradually so identifies himself with the former Eliezer's mythic role that he relates in the first person singular events that happened to that first Eliezer. In mythopoeic ages people have not yet an identity, only a role — if the role is identical, one self will easily merge into another.

Myth here is wrapped up in the art of the greatest storyteller of the age, an art maximally intense, beyond perfectibility, verging on the eerie. The magnificence of the formal artistry, the power of the portrayals cannot be expressed in the language of the literary historian trained to write simply and straightforwardly. It would be necessary to compose a panegyric of the kind with which the humanists of old expressed appreciation for each other's work — and perhaps they were right to do so.

Notes to Chapter 13

1. [First published in Antal Szerb, *Hétköznapok és csodák* (Budapest: Révai, 1936).]
2. [J. W. von Goethe, 'Selige Sehnsucht', ll. 17–20, trans. by Shinzen Young, <http://www.shinzen.org/Poetry/poemHolyLonging.htm> [accessed 18 July 2016] ('Und so lang du das nicht hast, | Dieses: Stirb und werde! | Bist du nur ein trüber Gast | Auf der dunklen Erde').]

3. [We now know that the work became a tetralogy and what Szerb refers to as the title of the second volume is that of the tetralogy as a whole. The 'second volume' is presumably what is now known as *The Young Joseph*.]

INDEX

Lightning Source UK Ltd.
Milton Keynes UK
UKHW030655120721
387033UK00006B/420